SIMPLY CLASSIC

The Junior League of Seattle

Editors	Kay Baxter Lucy Bauer Footlik	Sales and Promotion	Elizabeth Greathouse *Chairman*
Chairman	Kayce Stevens Hughlett *1992-1993*		Madeline Fish Linda Harrison Ellen Mooney
	Laura Halliday *1991-1992*		Susan Simonds Teri Woods
	Carol Smith *1989-1991*	Design	The Leonhardt Group Janet Kruse Barbara Ferguson
	Julie Bell *Administrative Assistant*	Illustration	Heidi-Marie Blackwell
	Anne Ossewaarde *Recipe Chairman*	Production	Lisa Zefkeles
	Barbara Ries *Nordstrom Liaison*	Calligraphy	Tim Young
	Terri Turnure *Cookbook Vice Chairman*	Copywriting	Kit Hutchin
	Betsy Wilcox *Assistant Editor*	Printing	Graphic Arts Center

Profits from the sale of this cookbook are used to support community projects of the Junior League of Seattle, Inc.

The Junior League of Seattle is an organization of women committed to promoting voluntarism, developing the potential of women, and improving the community through the effective action and leadership of trained volunteers. Its purpose is exclusively educational and charitable.

The Junior League of Seattle devotes more than 100,000 volunteer hours each year to community projects in the areas of education, the arts, human services, and family, children's and women's issues.

N

NORDSTROM

Simply Classic is proudly sponsored by Nordstrom. The Junior League of Seattle recognizes and thanks Nordstrom for its generous donation and support toward the publication of this book.

Acknowledgements

Cookbook Committee, 1991-1992

Betsy Amento
Kay Baxter
Jina Bonime
Sally Casey
Lucy Footlik
Elizabeth Greathouse
Laura Halliday
Kayce Hughlett

Bonnie Mickelson
Jamie Milne
Kay Nichols
Anne Ossewaarde
Barbara Ries
Cathy Rodden
Molly Smith
Terri Turnure

Cookbook Committee, 1990-1991

Helen Becker
Lou Bush
Cary Clark
Lucy Footlik
Laura Halliday
Claudia Hansen
Betsy LaTorre
Bonnie Mickelson
Terry Moos
Amy Rudolf

Betsy Silva
Susan Simmons
Carol Smith
Mary Smith
Ann Stables
Pam Stewart
Barb Sulman
Terri Turnure
Betsy Wilcox
Anne Willoughby

Cookbook Committee, 1989-1990

Margaret Bordeaux
Lou Bush
Melissa Evans
Linda MacGeorge

Jeva Marshall
Joy Murray
Carol Smith

Table of Contents

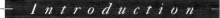

WELCOME TO SIMPLY CLASSIC

❖   In this collection of favorite recipes, the Junior League of Seattle celebrates our eclectic style of Northwest living and takes advantage of our proximity to some of the world's best seafood, some of the country's most prolific farms, ranches and orchards, one of the country's best farmers' markets and every kind of ethnic grocer you can imagine.

❖   Four years in the making, Simply Classic contains over 250 fabulous recipes, chosen from more than 2,000 submitted by Junior League of Seattle members, their families and friends. Every recipe was tested, retested, then tested again by enthusiastic League members and friends. Then our editors (excellent chefs in their own right) tested, refined and selected the recipes for utmost reliability.

❖   We've included quick and easy recipes for every day and some extravagant creations that pull out all the stops. Recipes that are light and healthy and the occasional indulgence. Recipes from around the world and some all-American classics. Recipes that are elegant and some that are just plain fun. Of course, they're all simply delicious.

❖   We've designed our book to be easy to handle and easy to use. We hope you reach for it often. Although we think it's beautiful now, we think it will look even better once you've added your own fingerprints and chocolate smudges. Enjoy!

Menus

NORTHWEST HARVEST DINNER

Menu Selection

Harvest Bisque *p. 40*

Pork Roast with Spicy Pears *p. 185*

Winter Wild Rice with Dried Cherries *p.213*

Wild Mushroom Sauté *p. 200*

Apple Bread Pudding with Cider Sauce *p.244*

❖ Under the glittering Seattle skyline, it's easy to forget that we're surrounded by hard-working farms. And orchards and wheat fields and fishing villages and dairies and berry fields and cranberry bogs and vineyards and cider presses and breweries. But in the exhilarating first crisp days of autumn, Seattle markets and street corners are burgeoning with the bounty of our spectacular state. Here's a menu to fill your kitchen with the robust and pungent aromas of fall.

SIMPLY CLASSIC DINNER

Menu Selection

Pesto Roast Chicken *p. 162*

Julienne of Carrots & Snowpeas *p. 198*

Parmesan Potato Wedges *p. 203*

Rosemary Biscuits *p. 56*

Apple Pie Americana *p. 238*

❖ These days it seems we're yearning for a return to the basics. For the comfort of the "meat-and-potatoes" classics that Mom used to make. But we're not willing to give up our own fresher, simpler, more worldly style of cooking. Here's a menu that offers the best of all worlds — wholesome ingredients, easy preparation, elegant international flourishes, old-fashioned satisfaction.

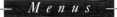

BEST OF THE MARKET DINNER

❖ Visitors to Seattle marvel at the Pike Place Market. Locals cherish it. Especially after nearly losing it to "urban renewal" in the 1960s. Between the colorful mosaics of produce at its high stalls, its fishmongers, butchers, bakers and dairies, its global ethnic specialty shops, and its wine merchants, you'd be hard pressed to name anything you can't find there. This menu will lead you on a treasure hunt that will remind you never to take our Market for granted.

SEATTLE SEAFOOD SAMPLER

❖ The sweet brine of freshly dug clams. The glint of salmon just off the boat. Whether you choose your seafood right off the deck of a trawler at Fisherman's Terminal, from your favorite fishmonger at the Market, or catch it yourself — this is the very best of West Coast living.

HERB GARDEN DINNER

❖   The Herbfarm in Fall City, with its little urban offshoots in Seattle, has inspired many a Seattle chef in the quiet revolution out of the spice jar and into the garden. Here, and at other local herb farms, you can buy starters or fill your basket with fresh-cut herbs. On the highway home, don't ignore the colorful hand-painted signs for Washington's roadside fruit stands and U-pick berry farms. Food doesn't get any fresher than this.

PICNIC AT THE WINERY

❖   A big checked blanket, a well-stocked wicker hamper, a spectacular view of the abundant vineyards — and good company. What a splendid way to wrap up a visit (and, of course, a comprehensive tasting!) at any one of Washington's famed wineries. Close your eyes in the midday sun — you might almost swear you were on a hillside in Tuscany. Salute!

SALMON BBQ ON THE BEACH

❖ Seattleites are known to squeeze every precious minute out of our long summer days. Here's a perfect way to celebrate the sunset on the Sound, the ocean or the lake. Prepare it all ahead, then gather 'round the coals and watch the ferries pass and the city light up.

HOME TEAM TAILGATE

❖ Where else in the country can football fans "tailgate" aboard their boats? At Husky Stadium, on the shore of Lake Washington, tailgating is no "sandwich and thermos" affair. Whether they arrive on a 60-foot yacht or in a rubber dinghy, Husky fans know how to celebrate. Here's a great make-ahead menu. The brownies are definitely a touchdown.

DINING ON DECK

❖   With more boats per capita than any other coastal city, most Seattleites know the ropes and are sure hands in the galley. Here's a menu that's fresh as the sea air and easy to take along for the ride. (Tip: If you don't have a boat — offer to bring lunch. We guarantee you'll be invited aboard again.)

BRUNCH ON THE PATIO

❖   People in Seattle know a good day when they see one. And they head out-of-doors. But it isn't all backpacks and bicycles. Here's an elegant midday menu to share with your city friends on your backyard patio or highrise roof-garden. The scones were inspired by the little inns and rooming houses all over Washington that have given our state a reputation for warm hospitality — a reputation this brunch is sure to enhance.

FIRESIDE DINNER

❖ Winter in Seattle usually means rain, rain and more rain! It makes us yearn for a storybook season. So we jump in the car, strap on the skis, and head east to a winter wonderland in the Cascade Mountains, barely an hour away. This hearty Italian feast is perfect by a roaring fire. Prepare the torta ahead, and go build a snowman. What's one more for dinner?

FLASH-IN-THE-PAN WEEKNIGHT DINNER

❖ It's Tuesday night. Your meeting ran late. Basketball practice starts at 7:00. Drama rehearsal's at 7:30. The committee is convening at your dining room table at 8:00. Just an average busy "day in the life." You're going to love this menu. Everything tastes so great, you'd think you spent the day in the kitchen. But it's so easy to put together, you might even get the kids to pitch in!

EAST MEETS WEST

❖ Poised on the edge of the continent, with a population as ethnically diverse as any city, Seattle is open to culinary influences from all over the world — especially the Pacific Rim. Our International District is home to some of the finest eastern cuisine on the West Coast. And our Asian grocery markets are an experience in themselves. Here's a menu that illustrates perfectly our Northwest knack for combining fresh local ingredients and international ideas in creative new ways. A word of warning — only true ginger fans need apply.

NORTHWEST OF THE BORDER FIESTA

❖ In this menu, Northwest meets Southwest for a colorful dinner that's perfect party fare. Let the festivities begin with a trip to the Market for ripe red tomatoes, jalapeño peppers, jicama, cilantro, fresh halibut, tortillas and juicy limes. Why not welcome your guests with the festive flickering of candlelight in brown paper luminarias? And top the evening off with a whack at a piñata. Olé!

RITES OF SPRING

❖   There is nothing quite like the freshness of Northwest spring air or the startling blue of a Seattle sky after a long, grey winter. The cherry blossoms, the daffodils, the longer days — it's almost mystical and certainly worth celebrating. Here's a menu that glorifies what, for many in Seattle, is the very best time of the year. Ellensburg spring lamb, Oregon hazelnuts, Yakima Valley asparagus, island wild berries. And, of course, one can't possibly have too many fresh Skagit Valley tulips on the table.

MAKE AHEAD PARTY BUFFET

❖   While parties in Seattle can be as elegant as in any world-class city, they're likely to be relaxed, too. Hosts and hostesses here pride themselves on their easy, casual approach to entertaining. No stuffed shirts in this crowd! Here's a dazzling buffet menu of dishes that taste as good as they look and leave you all the time in the world for the most important part of any party — your friends.

Dilled Grilled Prawns
18

Fireworks Clams
19

Broiled Mussels Pernod
20

Party Peppers & Shrimp
21

Pork & Peanut Skewers
22

Spicy Thai Beef Strips
23

Caesar Cream
24

Hearts of Palm Spread
25

Baked Curried Brie
25

Perfectly Pesto Cheesecake
26

Prosciutto Pinwheels
27

Olive Crostini
28

Won Ton Crisps
28

Vanilla Walnuts
29

Crunchy Glazed Pecans
29

Caponata
30

Pita Triangles
31

Fresh Tomato Bruschetta
32

Bootlegs
33

Sparkling Pineapple Sangria
33

DILLED GRILLED PRAWNS
makes twenty-four appetizers

Ingredients

24	bamboo skewers
24	large prawns
¼	cup white vermouth
¼	cup olive oil
2	tablespoons fresh parsley, chopped
2	tablespoons green onion, chopped
2	tablespoons fresh dill or 2 teaspoons dried
1	tablespoon Dijon mustard
1	medium clove garlic, minced
1	bay leaf
	freshly ground pepper

Marinating time 1 hour. Preheat grill.

❖ Cover bamboo skewers with hot water and soak 30 minutes or more. Peel and devein prawns. Skewer prawns and place in a shallow baking dish. Combine all other ingredients in a small bowl. Pour marinade over prawns, cover and refrigerate at least 1 hour or up to overnight.

❖ Remove prawns from marinade. Grill 1 to 2 minutes per side, or until barely opaque throughout. Serve hot or at room temperature.

FIREWORKS CLAMS
serves four

Ingredients

2	tablespoons olive oil
2	medium cloves garlic, minced
1	teaspoon oregano, dried
1/4	teaspoon red pepper flakes
1 1/2	cups fennel bulb, thinly sliced
1/2	cup onion, chopped
1	14-ounce can plum tomatoes, chopped
1/2	cup dry white wine
1/2	teaspoon fennel seeds
	salt and black pepper
1	pound small clams
2	tablespoons fresh parsley, chopped

❖ Heat olive oil in a large, deep sauté pan over medium-low heat. Add garlic, oregano and red pepper flakes. Cook, stirring often, for 1 minute. Add fennel and onion. Cook until fennel is soft, about 10 minutes. Add undrained tomatoes, wine and fennel seeds. Season to taste with salt and pepper. Simmer uncovered, stirring occasionally, 5 minutes.

❖ Discard any open clams that do not close when tapped. Scrub clams under cold running water. Add clams to pan, cover and steam until they open, about 5 minutes. Discard any clams that do not open. Transfer clams to a large serving dish and spoon tomato mixture over. Sprinkle with parsley and serve hot.

Fennel bulb has a mildly sweet, anise flavor. If fennel is not available, celery can be substituted in this dish.

BROILED MUSSELS PERNOD
makes six dozen mussels

Ingredients

6   dozen fresh mussels

½   cup white wine or dry vermouth (optional)

2   bay leaves

2   cloves garlic, peeled

1   cup butter or margarine, softened

2   tablespoons tomato paste

2   tablespoons Pernod

1   tablespoon lemon juice, freshly squeezed

1   teaspoon salt

½   teaspoon black pepper

¼   teaspoon nutmeg, freshly grated or ⅛ teaspoon ground

1   small Roma tomato or ½ small regular tomato, seeded and diced

⅓   cup fine, dry bread crumbs

2   tablespoons fresh parsley, chopped

Chilling time up to 24 hours.

❖ Debeard and scrub mussels. Steam mussels in a covered pan with about 2 inches of water, ½ cup white wine or vermouth and 2 bay leaves. Remove mussels from pan with tongs as soon as they open. Set aside. Discard any mussels that do not open. Remove half the shell from each mussel and discard. Place mussels on the half shell in a single layer in a broiler-proof baking pan. Set aside in the refrigerator.

❖ With machine running, drop garlic through feed tube of a food processor and mince finely. Add butter, tomato paste, Pernod, lemon juice, salt, pepper and nutmeg; blend well. Transfer mixture to a small bowl and fold in diced tomato by hand. This topping can be made ahead and stored for up to a week in the refrigerator or frozen for a month. (It is also good on clams or oysters.)

❖ Spread each mussel generously with butter mixture and sprinkle with bread crumbs, coating evenly. Chill well. It is best to prepare mussels several hours or a day ahead so topping is very well-chilled before broiling. If butter is not chilled when mussels are broiled, they tend to be greasy and will not develop a crisp crust.

❖ Just before serving, broil mussels until golden and bubbly. Sprinkle with parsley and serve warm.

PARTY PEPPERS & SHRIMP
serves ten

Ingredients

2	pounds jumbo shrimp
1	large red bell pepper
1	large green bell pepper
1	large yellow bell pepper
1	tablespoon olive oil
2	cups red onion, sliced
3	tablespoons capers, drained
	toasted baguette slices

Marinade

1 ½	cups vegetable oil
½	cup apple cider vinegar
½	cup tomato sauce
2	tablespoons Tabasco sauce
2	tablespoons Worcestershire sauce
1	tablespoon sugar
2	teaspoons dry mustard
1	teaspoon salt

Marinating time 8 to 48 hours. Preheat oven to 450°.

❖ For Shrimp: bring a large pan of water to a gentle boil. Peel and devein shrimp. Immerse shrimp in boiling water just until opaque throughout, about 2 minutes. Do not overcook or shrimp will become tough. Drain and run immediately under cold water. When completely cool, drain on paper towels.

❖ For Peppers: cut each pepper in half lengthwise and remove seeds. Flatten each half with palm of hand. Place peppers, skin side up, in a single layer on a baking sheet. Brush with olive oil. Roast peppers until skins blister and char all over, about 15 minutes. Remove from oven and place peppers in a plastic bag to steam for 10 minutes. Scrape off skin and cut peppers into thin strips.

❖ In a large bowl, combine shrimp, roasted peppers, onions and capers. Combine all marinade ingredients in a small bowl and mix well. Pour marinade over shrimp mixture and stir to coat evenly. Marinate, refrigerated, at least 8 hours or up to 2 days. Stir often during marinating. Serve with toasted baguette slices.

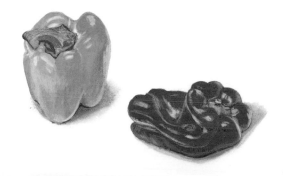

PORK & PEANUT SKEWERS
serves six

Ingredients

24   bamboo skewers

1   pound boneless pork tenderloin

½   cup lemon juice, freshly squeezed

¼   cup soy sauce

2   cloves garlic, minced

1   tablespoon brown sugar

1   teaspoon curry powder

      pinch of cayenne

Peanut Sauce

1   tablespoon peanut oil

½   cup green onion, chopped

1   tablespoon fresh ginger, minced

1   clove garlic, minced

1   teaspoon curry powder

¾   cup chicken stock

⅓   cup peanut butter

1   tablespoon lemon juice, freshly squeezed

1   tablespoon brown sugar

2   teaspoons soy sauce

¼   teaspoon red pepper flakes

Marinating time 2 to 24 hours. Preheat grill.

❖ For Pork: cover bamboo skewers with hot water and soak 1 hour or more. To aid in slicing, place meat in freezer 30 to 45 minutes. While still partially frozen, slice pork on the diagonal into thin strips, each about 3-inches long. Thread pork onto skewers, weaving skewers in and out of meat lengthwise, creating a serpentine effect. Place skewers in a shallow baking dish. In a small bowl, mix together lemon juice, soy sauce, garlic, brown sugar, curry powder and cayenne. Pour over pork, cover and marinate in refrigerator at least 2 hours or overnight. Turn occasionally during marinating.

❖ For Peanut Sauce: heat oil in a saucepan over medium heat. Add green onion and ginger. Cook until tender, about 5 minutes. Add garlic, cook 1 minute. Add curry powder, cook 1 minute, stirring constantly. Mix in remaining ingredients. Bring to a boil and stir until sauce thickens. Transfer to serving dish.

❖ Cook pork skewers on a medium-hot grill 4 to 6 minutes, turning several times. Brush often with marinade during cooking. Serve with warm peanut sauce for dipping.

SPICY THAI BEEF STRIPS
serves six

1 pound top sirloin or top round steak

1 head green leaf lettuce, cleaned

Marinade

¼ cup soy sauce

2 tablespoons Asian sesame oil

2 tablespoons green onion, chopped

2 medium cloves garlic, minced

2 teaspoons sesame seeds, toasted

1 teaspoon rice wine vinegar

½ teaspoon black pepper

¼ teaspoon cayenne

Marinating time 8 to 24 hours. Preheat grill.

❖ To aid in slicing, place meat in freezer 30 to 45 minutes. Using a long, sharp knife with a thin blade, slice meat into thin strips while still partially frozen.

❖ Combine all marinade ingredients in a small bowl and blend well. Pour marinade over sliced meat. Cover and marinate in refrigerator 8 hours or overnight. Stir occasionally during marinating.

❖ Remove meat from marinade. Transfer marinade to a small saucepan and simmer until slightly thickened. Cook beef strips on a medium-hot grill 1 to 2 minutes per side for medium-rare. Arrange meat on a serving platter with lettuce leaves on the side. Pour marinade over meat. To eat, place a strip of beef on a lettuce leaf, roll up and eat with fingers.

❖ Alternately, thread uncooked beef onto bamboo skewers that have been soaked in water, weaving skewer in and out of meat to create a serpentine effect. Grill skewers 1 to 2 minutes per side. Spoon sauce over skewers when cooked. Serve immediately.

CAESAR CREAM
serves twelve

Ingredients

2	medium cloves garlic
½	cup Parmesan cheese, grated
½	cup fresh parsley, packed
6	canned anchovy fillets
3	tablespoons lemon juice, freshly squeezed
1	cup sour cream
3-4	heads romaine lettuce

Parmesan Toasts

1	baguette
2	tablespoons olive oil
¼	cup Parmesan cheese, grated

❖ With machine running, drop garlic through feed tube of a food processor and mince. Add Parmesan, parsley, anchovies and lemon juice. Process into a paste. Transfer to a bowl and fold in sour cream. Clean and separate small inner leaves of romaine. Reserve large leaves for another use.

❖ For Parmesan Toasts: preheat oven to 350°. Cut baguette into thin slices using a serrated knife. Place slices on a baking sheet in a single layer. Bake until lightly toasted, about 10 minutes, turning once during cooking. Remove from oven. Brush slices on one side with olive oil and sprinkle with Parmesan cheese. Return to oven and bake until golden, about 3 minutes.

❖ To Serve: place Caesar Cream in a small bowl on a tray. Surround with romaine leaves and Parmesan Toasts for dipping. This dip is also delicious served with an assortment of raw vegetables.

To get the most juice from a lemon, bring it to room temperature before squeezing.

HEARTS OF PALM SPREAD
serves ten

1	14-ounce can hearts of palm
¾	cup Parmesan cheese, freshly grated
3	tablespoons green onion, finely chopped
⅔	cup mayonnaise
¼	cup sour cream
2	tablespoons pimiento, minced
⅛	teaspoon cayenne

Preheat oven to 350°.

❖ Drain hearts of palm and chop finely. Reserve 1 tablespoon each Parmesan and green onion. Mix hearts of palm thoroughly with remaining ingredients. Spread mixture into a shallow baking dish and sprinkle reserved Parmesan and green onion evenly over top. Bake 20 minutes or until hot and bubbly. Run quickly under broiler to brown top. Serve with toasted French bread slices, Pita Triangles (p.31) or crackers.

BAKED CURRIED BRIE
serves six

1	teaspoon curry powder
1	8-ounce wheel of Brie or Camembert
¼	cup fruit chutney
¼	cup cashews, coarsely chopped
	baguette slices or crackers

Preheat oven to 325°.

❖ Sprinkle curry over cheese. Using fingers, rub curry into top and sides. Spread chutney evenly over top and sprinkle with cashews. Gently press cashews into chutney so they adhere. Bake 7 to 10 minutes. If cheese is cold when placed in oven, add 5 minutes to cooking time. Transfer to serving platter and surround with baguette slices or crackers. Serve warm.

PERFECTLY PESTO CHEESECAKE
serves eighteen

Crust

1	tablespoon butter or margarine, softened
1/4	cup fine, dry bread crumbs
2	tablespoons Parmesan cheese, grated

Filling

2	8-ounce packages cream cheese, at room temperature
1	cup ricotta cheese
1/2	cup Parmesan cheese, grated
1/2	teaspoon salt
1/8	teaspoon cayenne
3	large eggs
1/2	cup pesto sauce
1/3	cup pine nuts

Garnish

fresh basil sprigs

crackers

Preheat oven to 325°.

❖ Rub butter or margarine over bottom and sides of a 9-inch diameter springform pan. Mix bread crumbs with 2 tablespoons grated Parmesan. Coat pan with crumb mixture.

❖ Using an electric mixer, beat cream cheese, ricotta, 1/2 cup Parmesan, salt, and cayenne until light and well blended. Add eggs one at a time, beating well after each addition. Transfer half the mixture to a medium bowl. Mix pesto into remaining half. Pour pesto mixture into prepared pan, smooth top. Carefully smooth plain cheese mixture over pesto mixture. Gently smooth top. Sprinkle with pine nuts.

❖ Bake cheesecake until center no longer moves when pan is shaken, about 45 minutes. Transfer to rack and cool completely. Run a small sharp knife around sides of pan to loosen cheesecake. Release pan sides from cheesecake. Transfer to platter, garnish with fresh basil sprigs, surround with crackers and serve.

❖ For a slightly different flavor, use the Spinach Pesto on page 116.

To keep pesto from turning black on top when stored, pour a thin film of olive oil over the surface, cover and refrigerate.

PROSCIUTTO PINWHEELS
makes twenty pinwheels

1   sheet frozen puff pastry, thawed

      flour for dusting

Filling

4   tablespoons sweet hot mustard

4   ounces Prosciutto, thinly sliced

1   cup Parmesan, freshly grated

Preheat oven to 350°. Chilling time 20 minutes.

❖   Dust work surface with flour and roll pastry sheet into a rectangle approximately 11x14 inches. Using a pastry brush, brush excess flour from surface of pastry. Spread mustard evenly over pastry, arrange prosciutto in a flat layer over mustard and sprinkle cheese evenly over all. Starting at long end, roll up pastry jelly-roll style until you reach the middle of the sheet. Roll the other half in the same manner until the two sides meet in the center. Place on a baking sheet and set a flat spatula or wooden spoon on each side to keep it from unrolling. Place in freezer until well chilled, at least 20 minutes. Can be made ahead up to this point and kept frozen, tightly wrapped, for up to 3 months.

❖   When ready to bake, slice partially thawed roll into ½-inch slices and place on a parchment-lined baking sheet. Bake 20 to 25 minutes or until puffed and golden. Serve warm or at room temperature.

Prosciutto is a ham that has been seasoned, salt cured and air dried. It is available in Italian markets and in the deli sections of some supermarkets.

OLIVE CROSTINI
makes twenty-four toasts

Ingredients

½	cup black olives
½	cup green olives with pimiento
2	medium cloves garlic
½	cup Parmesan, grated
4	tablespoons butter or margarine
2	tablespoons olive oil
½	cup Monterey Jack cheese, grated
¼	cup fresh parsley, chopped
1	baguette

Preheat oven to broil.

❖ Chop olives coarsely in food processor. Transfer to a medium bowl. With machine running, drop garlic through feed tube of food processor and mince. Add Parmesan, butter and olive oil. Process into a paste. Add butter mixture to bowl with olives. Fold in Monterey Jack and parsley. Mix well. Cut baguette into thin slices. Spread each slice generously with olive mixture. Cook under broiler until bubbly and lightly browned.

WON TON CRISPS
makes forty crisps

Ingredients

4	tablespoons butter or margarine
5	egg roll wrappers
½	cup Parmesan cheese, grated
	fresh or dried herbs such as basil, parsley, oregano or thyme (optional)

Preheat oven to 375°.

❖ Melt butter in a small saucepan or in microwave. Brush a baking sheet or jelly roll pan lightly with a small amount of melted butter. Brush egg roll wrappers on one side with remaining butter. Cut each egg roll wrapper into 4 squares, then cut each square in half, to make 8 rectangles. Place rectangles in a single layer on baking sheet. Sprinkle with cheese and optional herbs. Bake uncovered for 5 to 6 minutes or until golden. Repeat process until all won tons are baked.

VANILLA WALNUTS
makes one pound of nuts

Ingredients

1	pound walnut halves
3	tablespoons corn oil
1	tablespoon pure vanilla extract
½	cup sugar
¼	teaspoon ground coriander
¼	teaspoon cinnamon
¼	teaspoon nutmeg
¼	teaspoon allspice
¼	teaspoon salt
⅛	teaspoon white pepper

Preheat oven to 325°.

❖ Bring a large pan of water to a boil. Blanch walnuts 1 minute. Drain well. Transfer to a bowl. Blend corn oil with vanilla extract. Pour over hot nuts. Sprinkle in sugar and toss to mix well. Let stand 10 minutes. Arrange nuts on a rimmed baking tray. Bake 30 to 35 minutes until nuts are light brown and crispy. Stir nuts a few times during baking. Combine remaining ingredients in a small bowl. When nuts are done baking, transfer to a large bowl while still hot. Toss with seasoning mixture. Return to baking sheet and spread in a single layer to cool. Serve at room temperature.

CRUNCHY GLAZED PECANS
makes one pound of nuts

Ingredients

¼	cup butter or margarine
¼	cup light corn syrup
2	tablespoons water
1	teaspoon salt
1	pound pecans

Preheat oven to 250°.

❖ Line a baking sheet with foil. Combine butter, corn syrup, water and salt in a medium saucepan and bring to a boil. Add pecans and stir to completely coat nuts. Spread nuts evenly on lined baking sheet. Bake for 1 hour, stirring every 10 minutes. Cool and serve.

❖ These nuts are also wonderful in salads!

CAPONATA
serves ten

Ingredients

- 1 ½ pounds eggplant
- ½ cup olive oil
- 1 28-ounce can tomatoes, undrained
- 3 cups onion, sliced
- 2 cups green bell pepper, chopped
- 2 medium cloves garlic, minced
- ½ cup fresh parsley, chopped
- ½ cup black olives, halved
- ⅓ cup red wine vinegar
- 2 tablespoons sugar
- 2 tablespoons capers, drained
- 2 tablespoons tomato paste
- 2 teaspoons dried basil
- 1 teaspoon salt
- ½ teaspoon black pepper
- ½ cup pine nuts

Preheat oven to 350°.

❖ Peel eggplant and cut into 1-inch cubes. Heat oil in a large, heavy sauté pan over medium heat. Add eggplant, tomatoes, onion, green pepper and garlic. Cook until eggplant is tender, 20 to 30 minutes. Add remaining ingredients, except pine nuts. Simmer 15 minutes.

❖ Meanwhile, toast pine nuts in oven until golden, about 8 minutes. Sprinkle pine nuts over caponata just before serving. Serve at room temperature with Pita Triangles or baguette slices.

PITA TRIANGLES

makes seventy-two triangles

Ingredients

¾	cup butter, softened
2	tablespoons fresh parsley, minced
1	tablespoon fresh chives, minced
1	tablespoon lemon juice, freshly squeezed
1	medium clove garlic, minced
6	pita rounds

Sitting time 1 hour. Preheat oven to 450°.

❖ Combine all ingredients except pita loaves in a small bowl. Blend thoroughly. Cover and let sit at least 1 hour at room temperature. Cut pita rounds in half. Separate each half into 2 pieces. Spread pieces evenly with butter mixture. Cut each piece into 3 triangles. Arrange triangles on a baking sheet in a single layer. Bake until lightly browned and crisp, about 5 minutes.

Christmas in April

Through this one day event, volunteers renovate houses of elderly and disadvantaged citizens in the Seattle area. In 1992, the Junior League coordinated the renovation of more than 20 homes. That number will increase each year as the project develops.

FRESH TOMATO BRUSCHETTA
serves eight

Ingredients

4	large tomatoes
1	cup mozzarella, finely diced
1/3	cup fresh basil, chopped
3	medium cloves garlic, minced
2	tablespoons fresh parsley, chopped
2	tablespoons olive oil
1/2	teaspoon salt
1/2	teaspoon black pepper
1	loaf crusty Italian bread
3	cloves garlic

Draining time 30 minutes. Prepare grill or preheat oven to broil.

❖   Cut tomatoes in half horizontally and squeeze out seeds. Cut tomato into very small dice. Place in a colander and drain 30 minutes. Transfer tomatoes to a bowl and add next 7 ingredients.

❖   Cut bread into ½-inch slices. Lightly crush garlic cloves with the side of a large knife or cleaver. Remove peel. Rub bread with garlic cloves. Toast both sides of bread on grill or under broiler.

❖   To Serve: transfer tomato mixture to a small serving bowl placed in the center of a platter. Surround with toasted bread and allow guests to serve themselves. Alternately, spread some tomato mixture on each slice of bread, arrange on a platter and serve.

This recipe works best with very ripe tomatoes. Try it in late summer when vine-ripened tomatoes are abundant.

BOOTLEGS
makes twelve cocktails

Bootleg Mix

1 12-ounce can frozen lemonade concentrate

1½ cups water

1½ cups fresh mint leaves

  vodka, rum, gin, or bourbon

  club soda

Ingredients

¼ cup lemon juice, freshly squeezed

¼ cup orange juice, freshly squeezed

2 tablespoons sugar

2 cups pineapple juice

2 cups dry white wine

1½ cups sparkling water

Garnish

1 lemon, thinly sliced

1 small orange, thinly sliced

4 medium strawberries, hulled and sliced

  mint sprigs, ice

❖ For Bootleg Mix: combine lemonade concentrate, water and mint leaves in a blender. Blend at high speed 15 to 30 seconds, until frothy. Spoon off froth and discard. Strain mixture through a fine sieve.

❖ Combine 2 ounces bootleg mix with 2 ounces vodka, rum, gin or bourbon and 4 ounces club soda. Serve over ice.

SPARKLING PINEAPPLE SANGRIA
serves eight

❖ In a large pitcher combine lemon juice, orange juice and sugar. Stir to dissolve sugar. Add pineapple juice, wine and sparkling water; stir. Garnish with lemon slices, orange slices, strawberries and mint. Serve over ice.

Bootleg mix is also good with straight club soda or added to ice tea.

White Gazpacho
36

Chilled Red Pepper Soup
36

Hot or Cold Leek Soup
37

Gingered Carrot Soup
38

Garden Fresh Zucchini Soup
38

Roasted Eggplant Soup
39

Harvest Bisque
40

Sherried Split Pea Soup
40

Fresh Mushroom Soup
41

Cream of Any Green Soup
42

Artichoke & Scallop Chowder
43

More Than Minestrone
44

Spicy Black Bean Soup with Shrimp
45

Rainy Day Beef & Barley Soup
46

Mount Rainier Chili
47

Lentil Soup with Sausage
48

Cascade Chicken Noodle Soup
49

Seattle Seafood Stew
50

Fiesta Corn Soup
51

WHITE GAZPACHO
serves six

2	cucumbers, peeled and seeded
1	medium clove garlic
1¼	cups chicken stock
1¼	cups sour cream
2	teaspoons rice vinegar
1	teaspoon salt
¼	cup tomato, seeded and diced
¼	cup chives, minced

Chilling time 1 hour.

❖ Cut cucumbers into 2-inch chunks. Place cucumber and garlic in processor or blender and blend until evenly pureed. Add chicken stock, sour cream, vinegar and salt. Mix briefly, just to blend. Chill 1 hour. Pour soup into serving bowls, sprinkle with chopped tomato and chives. Serve immediately.

CHILLED RED PEPPER SOUP
serves six

Ingredients

2	tablespoons butter or margarine
2	large red bell peppers, roasted, peeled and chopped
2	cups onion, chopped
¾	cup chicken stock
2	cups buttermilk
½	teaspoon Tabasco sauce

Garnish

chili powder

Chilling time 4 hours.

❖ In a heavy, 3-quart saucepan, melt butter over medium heat. Sauté peppers and onion until tender but not browned. Add chicken stock, cover and simmer 30 minutes.

❖ Drain liquid from vegetables and reserve in a large bowl. Place vegetables in a food processor or blender and puree. Stir pureed vegetables into reserved liquid. Stir in buttermilk and Tabasco. Cover and chill for 4 hours. Serve chilled, garnished with a sprinkle of chili powder.

HOT OR COLD LEEK SOUP

serves six

Ingredients

1	large leek
2	tablespoons olive oil
1	cup onion, chopped
6	cups chicken stock
1½	pounds potatoes, peeled and cut into 2-inch dice
½	teaspoon salt
½	teaspoon white pepper
2½	cups milk
½	teaspoon Tabasco sauce (optional)
6	tablespoons fresh chives, minced

Chilling time 1 hour.

❖ Split leek in half lengthwise and cut each half into ¼-inch pieces. Clean leek by immersing the pieces in a bowl filled with cold water. Remove from water and drain in a sieve.

❖ Heat oil in a large heavy pot. Add leek and onion, cover and cook over medium-low heat for 5 minutes, until soft and slightly brown. Add stock, potatoes, salt and pepper. Bring to a boil. Reduce heat and simmer for 20 to 25 minutes, until potatoes are tender.

❖ Strain liquid from soup into a bowl and reserve. Place solids in food processor and blend briefly, just until pureed. Gradually mix in reserved liquid. Slowly stir milk into soup mixture, until smooth.

❖ To serve hot, reheat soup over medium heat about 7 minutes, until steamy. To serve chilled, stir in Tabasco sauce and refrigerate at least 1 hour. Sprinkle with chopped chives before serving.

GINGERED CARROT SOUP
serves six

Ingredients

1	tablespoon butter or margarine
½	cup onion, chopped
2	cloves garlic, minced
5	cups carrots, thinly sliced
1	tablespoon fresh ginger, minced
4	cups chicken stock
¼	cup lime juice
	plain yogurt
	chives, chopped

❖ Melt butter in a large heavy pot over medium-low heat. Add onion and sauté until tender, but not browned, about 10 minutes. Add garlic, cook 3 minutes more. Stir in carrots and ginger. Add chicken stock and simmer until carrots are tender, about 20 minutes. Add lime juice and puree soup in blender until smooth.

❖ Chill or serve warm, topped with a dollop of yogurt and a sprinkle of herbs.

GARDEN FRESH ZUCCHINI SOUP
serves six

Ingredients

5	medium zucchini
3	large carrots
1	cup onion, chopped
4	cups chicken stock
1	8-ounce package cream cheese
½	teaspoon salt
¼ - ½	teaspoon white pepper

❖ Cut zucchini and carrots into 1-inch slices. Combine with onion and chicken stock in a large, heavy pot. Cover and bring to a boil. Reduce heat and simmer until vegetables are tender-crisp, about 7 minutes.

❖ Place half of vegetable mixture and half of cream cheese in blender or processor and blend until smooth. Place the pureed mixture in a bowl. Repeat with remaining vegetables and cheese; add to soup in bowl. Stir in salt and white pepper.

❖ Delicious served either hot or cold.

ROASTED EGGPLANT SOUP

serves six

Ingredients

2	medium eggplants
2	tablespoons vegetable oil, divided
4	medium cloves garlic, minced
2	cups onion, chopped
8	cups chicken stock
1	6-ounce can tomato paste
1	cup fresh basil leaves or $\frac{1}{4}$ cup dried basil
$\frac{1}{2}$	teaspoon salt
$\frac{1}{4}$	teaspoon pepper

Preheat broiler.

❖   Cut each eggplant in half lengthwise and place on oiled baking sheets, skin side up. Rub skin with 1 tablespoon oil and place under broiler. Broil until skins are charred and blistered, 10 to 15 minutes. Allow to cool.

❖   Peel eggplant and cut into chunks. Heat remaining tablespoon oil in a large skillet. Add eggplant, garlic and onion. Sauté until vegetables are softened, about 15 minutes.

❖   Place chicken stock in a large, heavy pot over medium heat. Add sautéed vegetables, tomato paste, basil, salt and pepper. Simmer about 15 minutes. Puree soup in batches in a food processor or blender.

❖   Return soup to pot and simmer gently until heated through. Serve immediately.

Another way to roast an eggplant is to rub it with oil and place it directly over the medium-high flame of a gas burner. Turn until all sides are charred.

HARVEST BISQUE
serves six

1	pound butternut squash
5	cups chicken stock
4	tablespoons butter
4	tablespoons flour
1	teaspoon curry powder
¾	cup half and half
1	tablespoon lime juice
½	teaspoon salt
¼	teaspoon white pepper

Garnish

1	lime, sliced paper thin

❖ Peel, seed, and cut squash into 1-inch cubes. Place in a heavy, 4-quart pot with chicken stock. Cook over medium heat until tender, about 15 minutes. Using a slotted spoon, transfer squash to a blender or food processor. Blend until smooth. Stir stock into squash puree. Set aside.

❖ In same pot, melt butter; stir in flour and curry. Cook, stirring, over medium heat until smooth. Add pureed squash mixture to pot. Increase heat to medium-high and stir until soup thickens slightly. Reduce heat and add half and half. Do not allow soup to boil after this point. Add lime juice, salt and white pepper. Ladle soup into serving bowls, garnish with lime and serve immediately.

SHERRIED SPLIT PEA SOUP
serves six

Ingredients

2	cups dried split peas
7	cups chicken stock
¼	cup dry sherry
¼	cup lemon juice
1	large bay leaf
1	teaspoon cumin
½	teaspoon salt
¼	teaspoon dry mustard
¼	teaspoon chili powder
¼	teaspoon cinnamon

❖ In a large, heavy pot, combine peas and chicken stock. Bring to a boil. Reduce heat and simmer, uncovered, for 60 minutes. Stir occasionally, mashing peas as you stir.

❖ Add sherry, lemon juice, bay leaf, cumin, salt, dry mustard, chili powder and cinnamon. Cover and cook over low heat for 20 minutes to allow flavors to blend. Remove bay leaf and serve immediately.

FRESH MUSHROOM SOUP
serves six

Ingredients

2	tablespoons butter, divided
2	tablespoons olive oil, divided
1	cup onion, chopped
1	medium clove garlic, minced
1	pound mushrooms, thickly sliced
6	cups chicken stock
1	cup dry white wine
3	tablespoons tomato paste
	salt and pepper to taste
1/4	cup fresh parsley, minced

❖   Melt 1 tablespoon butter in a large, heavy pot. Add 1 tablespoon olive oil and the onion. Sauté over medium-low heat, stirring often, until onion softens. Do not brown. Add garlic and cook 2 minutes more. Remove onion and garlic from pot and set aside. Melt remaining butter in same pot. Add remaining olive oil and mushrooms. Sauté over medium heat, stirring often, until mushrooms begin to soften and release their juices. Add chicken stock, wine, tomato paste and reserved onion mixture. Bring to a boil, reduce heat and simmer gently for 15 minutes. Add salt and pepper, if desired. Stir in fresh parsley and serve immediately.

For more exotic flavor, chanterelle or shitake mushrooms may replace half of the mushrooms in this recipe.

CREAM OF ANY GREEN SOUP
serves six

Ingredients

1	tablespoon vegetable oil
½	cup onion, chopped
4	cups chicken stock
¼	cup butter or margarine
¼	cup flour
½	teaspoon salt
¼	teaspoon white pepper
3	cups milk or half and half

Vegetable Choices

Cream of artichoke

2¼	cups artichoke hearts, rinsed
	chopped parsley for garnish

Cream of asparagus

5	cups asparagus, cut into 1-inch pieces
1½	teaspoons lemon juice
¼	teaspoon tarragon leaves, crumbled
	reserved asparagus tips for garnish

❖ Heat oil in large saucepan and sauté onion over medium-low heat until soft but not brown, about 5 minutes. Add chicken stock, vegetables and appropriate seasonings. Simmer over medium heat until vegetables are tender. (Timing will vary depending upon the vegetable. Broccoli and cauliflower will take longer than asparagus, peas, artichokes and spinach.) When vegetables are soft, place about ⅓ of the soup mixture in a blender or processor with metal blade inserted and process until mixture is smooth. Repeat with remaining soup until all is pureed. Stir in appropriate cheese or ham, cover and set aside.

❖ Melt butter in a heavy, 8-quart pot over medium-low heat. Slowly blend in flour, salt and white pepper. Cook, stirring to form a smooth paste, just until mixture starts to turn golden. Add milk slowly, stirring constantly. Cook until mixture thickens. Add vegetable puree and cook, stirring, until heated through.

❖ Ladle soup into bowls, garnish and serve immediately.

Cream of broccoli

5   cups broccoli florets
1   teaspoon thyme, crumbled
½   cup Gruyère cheese, grated
     additional Gruyère for garnish

Cream of cauliflower

5   cups cauliflower florets
¾   teaspoon curry
1   cup cheddar cheese, shredded
     chopped chives for garnish

Cream of pea

4   cups fresh or frozen peas
¼   cup shredded lettuce
1¼   cups cooked ham, diced
     chopped chives for garnish

Cream of spinach

6   cups spinach leaves, packed
¼   teaspoon ground nutmeg
     chopped chives for garnish

ARTICHOKE & SCALLOP CHOWDER
serves six

Ingredients

3   tablespoons butter
1   cup red onion, finely chopped
2   tablespoons lemon juice, freshly squeezed
3   cups clam juice
3   cups heavy cream
1½   cups canned or frozen artichoke hearts, diced
2½   pounds bay scallops
¼   teaspoon salt
¼   teaspoon white pepper
⅛   teaspoon cayenne
1   tablespoon fresh chives, snipped

❖ In a large, heavy pot, melt butter over medium heat. Add onion and cook just until translucent, about 3 minutes. Add lemon juice and simmer until evaporated. Add clam juice, cream, artichokes and scallops. Simmer gently about 4 minutes. Do not boil. Season with salt, pepper and cayenne. Ladle soup into heated bowls. Garnish with snipped chives. Serve immediately.

MORE THAN MINESTRONE
serves six

5   slices bacon, cut into bite-sized pieces

1   cup onion, chopped

2   celery stalks, chopped

1   small carrot, chopped

3   medium cloves garlic, minced

1   28-ounce can peeled Italian-style tomatoes

½   cup fresh parsley, chopped

6   cups chicken stock

1   10-ounce can red kidney beans, drained and rinsed

1   10-ounce can cannellini white beans (or great Northern beans), drained and rinsed

1   9-ounce can garbanzo beans, drained and rinsed

1   teaspoon dried basil, crushed

1   teaspoon dried oregano, crushed

1 ½ cups small seashell-shaped pasta

     Parmesan cheese

❖ Sauté bacon in a large, heavy pot for 5 minutes, until just crisp. Add onion and celery to bacon and drippings. Cook until vegetables are soft, but not brown, about 5 minutes.

❖ Add carrot and minced garlic; cook 2 minutes longer. Add tomatoes, parsley, chicken stock, beans, basil and oregano. Simmer over medium heat for 20 minutes, stirring occasionally. Add the pasta shells and cook for 8 minutes longer, or until pasta is al dente. Stir frequently to prevent pasta from sticking. Additional liquid (stock or water) may be added if soup becomes too thick.

❖ Ladle into bowls and sprinkle with freshly grated Parmesan cheese.

This hearty soup freezes very well and the flavor improves with reheating.

SPICY BLACK BEAN SOUP WITH SHRIMP

serves six

Soup

2	cups dried black (turtle) beans, rinsed
3	tablespoons butter
2	tablespoons vegetable oil, divided
2	cups onion, finely chopped
4	medium cloves garlic, minced
2	teaspoons fresh ginger, minced
1/2	medium jalapeño pepper, minced
1	28-ounce can plum tomatoes, drained and coarsely chopped
2	teaspoons dried thyme
6-8	cups chicken stock
2	teaspoons salt
1/2	teaspoon pepper
24	medium shrimp, peeled and deveined
3	tablespoons cilantro leaves, chopped

Garlic Yogurt

1 1/2	cups plain yogurt
2	medium cloves garlic, minced

Soaking time overnight.

❖ For Soup: place beans in a large, heavy pot with enough water to cover by 3 inches. Let soak at room temperature overnight, drain and rinse.

❖ Heat butter and 1 tablespoon oil in same pot over medium-low heat. Add onion, garlic, ginger and jalapeño. Sauté until softened, about 5 minutes. Add drained beans, tomatoes, thyme and 6 cups chicken stock. Bring to a boil. Reduce heat, cover and simmer until beans are tender, 2 to 2 1/2 hours. Add more stock as necessary during this time. Transfer half of cooked beans to a food processor and puree. Return puree to remaining soup in pan. Add salt and pepper. Cover and keep warm. (Or refrigerate up to 2 days.)

❖ Heat remaining 1 tablespoon of oil in skillet. Add shrimp and sauté quickly, only until opaque and pink, about 3 minutes.

❖ For Garlic Yogurt: mix yogurt and garlic together in a non-reactive bowl. (Can be covered and refrigerated for up to 1 day.)

❖ To Serve: re-warm soup over low heat if necessary. Ladle into warm bowls and place four shrimp atop each. Add a dollop of yogurt and a few cilantro leaves. Serve immediately.

RAINY DAY BEEF & BARLEY SOUP
serves eight

Ingredients

1 ½	pounds beef round steak, trimmed of excess fat and cut into ½-inch cubes
¾	teaspoon salt
½	teaspoon pepper
2	tablespoons vegetable oil, divided
2	cups onion, finely chopped
1	cup carrot, diced
½	cup celery, chopped
1	pound mushrooms, sliced
1	teaspoon garlic, minced
¼	teaspoon dried thyme
1	14½-ounce can beef broth
1	14½-ounce can chicken broth
½	cup pearl barley
3	tablespoons fresh parsley, chopped

❖ Sprinkle beef with salt and pepper. Place 1 tablespoon oil in Dutch oven and brown beef until no longer pink. Transfer to a bowl. Heat remaining oil in same pot; add onion, carrot and celery. Cook, stirring, until vegetables are softened, about 5 minutes. Stir in mushrooms, garlic and thyme; cook 5 minutes more. Combine beef and chicken broths with enough water to equal 6 cups. Add to pot along with barley and beef. Bring to a boil, reduce heat, cover and simmer until beef is tender, about 1½ hours. Add more water, if necessary, during this cooking time. Sprinkle with parsley just before serving.

MOUNT RAINIER CHILI
serves twelve to fourteen

Ingredients

1	pound Great Northern white beans, rinsed and picked over
2	pounds boneless chicken breasts
1	tablespoon vegetable oil
2	cups onion, chopped
4	medium garlic cloves, minced
2	4-ounce cans chopped mild green chiles
2	teaspoons ground cumin
1½	teaspoons dried oregano, crumbled
¼	teaspoon ground cloves
¼	teaspoon cayenne
8	cups chicken stock
1	12-ounce can beer
3	cups Monterey Jack cheese, shredded and divided
	sour cream
	salsa
	fresh cilantro leaves, chopped

Soaking time overnight.

❖　Place beans in a large, heavy pot. Add enough cold water to cover by at least 3 inches. Cover and soak overnight.

❖　Place chicken in a large, heavy saucepan. Add cold water to cover and bring to a simmer. Cook until just tender, about 15 minutes. Drain and cool. Remove skin and cut chicken into cubes.

❖　Drain beans into large colander. Heat oil in same pot. Add onions and sauté over medium-low heat until translucent, about 10 minutes. Stir in garlic, green chiles, cumin, oregano, cloves and cayenne. Sauté 2 minutes. Add beans and stock. Bring to a boil. Reduce heat and simmer until beans are very tender, stirring occasionally, about 3 to 4 hours. Add additional water if necessary. (Can be prepared 1 day ahead. Cover and bring to a simmer before continuing.) Add chicken, beer and 1 cup of cheese. Stir until cheese melts. Ladle chili into bowls. Serve with remaining cheese, sour cream, salsa and cilantro leaves to sprinkle on top.

To quick-soak beans, add enough water to cover by 3 inches. Bring to boil, cover and remove from heat. Soak for 2 hours.

LENTIL SOUP WITH SAUSAGE
serves six

Ingredients

1	tablespoon olive oil
1	pound mild Italian sausage links, cut into ½-inch slices
8	ounces smoked ham, finely chopped
1	cup green bell pepper, diced
1	cup onion, chopped
1	medium carrot, diced
2	medium cloves garlic, minced
1	bay leaf
¼	teaspoon dried thyme, crumbled
9	cups chicken stock
1	15½-ounce can peeled whole tomatoes
1¼	cup dried lentils
	salt and pepper to taste
12	large spinach leaves, trimmed and shredded

❖   Heat olive oil in a large, heavy pot. Add sliced sausage and cook over medium heat for 8 to 10 minutes. Remove from pot. Drain off all but 2 tablespoons drippings and add ham, green pepper, onion and carrot to the pan. Cover and cook 10 minutes over medium-low heat. Add garlic, bay leaf and thyme. Cover and cook 5 minutes more.

❖   Return cooked sausage to the pan, along with chicken stock, tomatoes and lentils. Reduce heat to low, partially cover and simmer soup gently for about 1 hour.

❖   Skim fat from surface of soup and season with salt and freshly ground pepper to taste. Just before serving, stir in shredded spinach leaves.

CASCADE CHICKEN NOODLE SOUP
serves eight

Ingredients

2	tablespoons vegetable oil
1	cup onion, chopped
3	medium cloves garlic, minced
10	cups chicken stock
1	teaspoon dried thyme, crumbled
¼	teaspoon dried dill
¼	teaspoon pepper
5	sprigs parsley
2	carrots, sliced
6	ounces wide egg noodles
1	pound cooked chicken breast, cubed
2	tablespoons cornstarch
2	cups unflavored yogurt
¼	cup green onion, chopped

❖ Heat oil in a large, heavy pot. Add onion and cook over medium-low heat until onion is soft, about 10 minutes. Add garlic and cook 2 minutes longer. Stir in chicken stock, thyme, dill, pepper, parsley and carrots. Cover and bring to a boil. Reduce heat and simmer 20 minutes. Remove and discard parsley; add noodles to stock. Simmer, uncovered, over medium-high heat until noodles are soft, about 10 minutes. Add chicken and cover pot to keep soup hot. In a small bowl, stir cornstarch into yogurt, then combine with 1 cup of hot broth. Return this mixture to soup pot and bring to a boil while stirring constantly. Remove from heat and serve immediately, garnished with green onion.

SEATTLE SEAFOOD STEW

serves six

Ingredients

½	cup olive oil
3	medium cloves garlic, minced
1	cup each, onion, celery, fennel bulb, finely chopped
4	cups chicken stock
2	cups dry white wine
1	cup clam juice
2	15-ounce cans diced tomatoes, undrained
1	tablespoon tomato paste
1	teaspoon pepper
1	teaspoon each, saffron threads, fennel seed, crushed
½	teaspoon thyme
¼	teaspoon dried red pepper flakes, crushed
1	pound clams
1	pound mussels
1	pound large shrimp
1	pound firm fish (cod, snapper, sea bass)
1	tablespoon Pernod (optional)
½	cup parsley, minced

❖ In a heavy 8-quart pot, combine oil, garlic, onion, celery and fennel. Sauté until softened, about 7 minutes. Add chicken stock, wine, clam juice, tomatoes, tomato paste, pepper, saffron, fennel seed, thyme and red pepper flakes. Simmer 45 minutes.

❖ Clean clams and debeard mussels. Discard any open shells which do not close when tapped. Shell and devein shrimp. Cut fish into 1-inch pieces.

❖ In a heavy saucepan, place clams in 2 inches of water. Cover and cook over high heat 5 minutes. Add mussels to pan; cover and cook 3 minutes more. Discard any unopened shells. Add clams and mussels to large pot. Strain cooking liquid and add to pot along with shrimp, fish, Pernod and parsley. Simmer 5 minutes longer until shrimp is pink and fish is opaque. Serve immediately.

Prepare the broth earlier in the day, then cook the seafood just before serving. Don't forget a loaf of warm, crusty bread for soaking up the flavorful broth.

FIESTA CORN SOUP
serves six

Ingredients

1	tablespoon butter or margarine
1	cup onion, chopped
1	medium clove garlic, minced
2	17-ounce cans creamed corn
1	17-ounce can corn kernels
1	cup chicken stock
2	cups whole milk
1	4 ounce can green chiles, diced
1	teaspoon ground cumin
1	teaspoon ground white pepper
¼	teaspoon Tabasco sauce
2	cups chicken breast, cooked and cubed
1½	cups Monterey Jack cheese, shredded

Garnishes

black olives; sour cream; salsa; avocado, diced; tortilla chips, crumbled

❖ In a large, heavy pot, melt butter and sauté onion over medium heat until translucent, about 6 minutes. Add garlic and cook 2 minutes longer. Do not allow onion and garlic to brown.

❖ Puree creamed corn, corn kernels and chicken stock in a blender or food processor. The mixture should not be completely smooth, but should still have some texture. Add corn mixture to pot, and simmer gently over medium heat for 10 minutes. Stir in milk, green chiles, cumin, white pepper and Tabasco. Add chicken and shredded cheese; stir until cheese melts. Ladle into soup bowls. Serve immediately with your choice of garnishes.

Individual soup bowls may be lined with a warm tortilla before ladling in the soup. Place colorful garnishes in bowls to pass at the table.

Herbed Parmesan Muffins	*Bed & Breakfast Scones*
54	64
Chive Popovers	*Sleep-over Coffee Cake*
55	65
Rosemary Biscuits	*Berry Best Muffins*
56	66
Ranch House Bread	*Eggnog Muffins*
57	67
Walnut Herb Bread	*Cloud Cakes*
58	68
Focaccia Romana	*Pumpkin Puff Pancakes*
59	69
English Muffin Loaves	*Tomato & Basil Tart*
60	70
Quick Honey Whole-Wheat Bread	*Savory Cheddar Pie*
61	71
Sailor's Skillet Bread	*Take Along Frittata*
62	72
Sour Cherry Almond Bread	*Torte Milan*
63	73

HERBED PARMESAN MUFFINS
makes twelve muffins

Ingredients

2	cups flour
1	teaspoon sugar
2	teaspoons baking powder
$^1/_2$	teaspoon dried oregano leaves, crumbled
$^1/_2$	teaspoon dried basil leaves, crumbled
$^1/_4$	teaspoon garlic powder
$^1/_2$	teaspoon baking soda
$^1/_2$	teaspoon salt
1	cup Parmesan cheese, freshly grated
$^1/_2$	cup fresh basil, parsley or cilantro leaves, chopped
$1^1/_2$	cups buttermilk
$^1/_4$	cup olive oil
1	large egg

Preheat oven to 400°.

❖ In a medium bowl, combine flour, sugar, baking powder, seasonings, baking soda and salt. Mix until well-blended. Stir in Parmesan cheese and fresh herb of your choice.

❖ In a large bowl, combine buttermilk, oil and egg until well-blended. Stir in flour mixture until just moistened. Spoon into 12 paper-lined muffin cups.

❖ Bake 20 minutes in preheated oven until golden brown and a wooden pick inserted in center comes out clean. Cool in pan 10 minutes. Serve warm.

Pre-grated Parmesan cheese is available, but the flavor cannot compare to that of freshly grated.

CHIVE POPOVERS
makes ten popovers

Ingredients

1	tablespoon oil
1	cup flour
¼	teaspoon salt
1	cup milk
2	large eggs
2	tablespoons fresh chives, minced

Preheat oven to 450°.

❖ Oil 10 muffin cups and place in preheating oven while preparing batter.

❖ In a small bowl, combine flour and salt. In blender or processor, combine milk, eggs and chives. Blend well. Add dry ingredients and blend for 3 minutes.

❖ Remove muffin tin from oven and immediately pour in batter. Place in oven and bake 15 minutes. Reduce oven heat to 350° and bake an additional 10 minutes. Do not open oven door or popovers may fall. Remove from oven and pierce gently with a small, sharp knife to prevent collapsing. Serve warm with butter.

CPS

Child Protective Services is an integral part of King County's program for abused children. A grant from the Junior League in 1964 was fundamental in creating this important service.

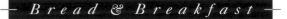

ROSEMARY BISCUITS
makes twelve biscuits

Ingredients

2	cups unbleached flour
1 ½	tablespoons baking powder
1	tablespoon sugar
½	teaspoon salt
1	tablespoon fresh rosemary leaves, crumbled or 1 ½ teaspoons dried
½	cup butter or margarine, softened
1	large egg, lightly beaten
¾	cup buttermilk

Preheat oven to 425°.

❖ In a large bowl, sift together dry ingredients. Add rosemary.

❖ Cut in butter with a pastry cutter or fingertips until crumbly. Stir together egg and buttermilk. Add to dry ingredients and stir until evenly moistened.

❖ Turn dough onto a floured board. Knead by hand about 5 minutes. Roll the dough into golf ball-sized portions and place 1 ½ inches apart on an ungreased cookie sheet. Place on middle rack of preheated oven and bake for 12 to 15 minutes until lightly browned on top. Serve warm.

RANCH HOUSE BREAD
makes two loaves

2	cups oatmeal, cooked on the dry side
5	tablespoons honey
2	tablespoons butter or margarine
1 ½	teaspoons salt
2	tablespoons active dry yeast
½	cup lukewarm milk (105° to 115°)
3 ½	cups unbleached flour
3	tablespoons sunflower seeds
3	tablespoons walnuts, chopped
1	large egg
1	tablespoon water
4	tablespoons uncooked rolled oats

Rising time 1 hour 30 minutes. Preheat oven to 375°.

❖ In a large mixing bowl, mix warm oatmeal with honey and butter. Add salt and stir well to combine.

❖ In a small bowl, combine yeast and lukewarm milk. Let stand 15 minutes or until yeast becomes foamy. Stir into oatmeal mixture. Add 1 cup flour, sunflower seeds and walnuts; stir to combine well. Gradually add 2 ¼ to 2 ½ cups flour and knead by hand or with a dough hook attachment on a heavy-duty mixer for about 10 minutes. The dough should be soft, but not sticky. Place dough in a large, greased bowl and turn to coat top and sides. Cover with oiled plastic wrap and let rise in a warm place for 1 hour, until doubled in bulk.

❖ Punch dough down, form into 2 loaves and place in 2 well-greased 9x5-inch loaf pans. Let rise, covered loosely with oiled plastic wrap, for 30 minutes until almost doubled in bulk. Brush with an egg wash, made by beating one egg together with 1 tablespoon water. Gently press two tablespoons uncooked rolled oats onto top of each loaf. Bake in preheated oven 45 to 50 minutes until loaves are nicely browned. Turn out from pan and let cool on a wire rack before slicing.

WALNUT HERB BREAD
makes two loaves

1 package active dry yeast

2 tablespoons brown sugar, divided

¼ cup lukewarm water (105° to 115°)

5½ cups unbleached or bread flour

1 tablespoon salt

2 cups lukewarm water (105° to 115°)

3 tablespoons walnut oil

½ cup walnuts or hazelnuts, toasted and chopped

½ cup fresh parsley leaves, chopped

2 tablespoons fresh basil, minced

2 tablespoons fresh oregano, minced

2 tablespoons fresh dill, minced

2 tablespoons lemon zest, grated

Rising time 2 hours 30 minutes. Preheat oven to 375°.

❖   In a small bowl, sprinkle yeast and a pinch of brown sugar over ¼ cup lukewarm water. Stir to dissolve and let stand until foamy, about 10 minutes.

❖   In a large bowl of electric mixer, combine 1 cup flour, remaining brown sugar and salt. Add 2 cups warm water, yeast mixture and oil. Beat on medium speed until smooth, about 2 minutes. Add remaining flour ½ cup at a time, until dough becomes stiff.

❖   Turn out onto a lightly floured surface and knead until smooth (about 5 minutes), working in chopped nuts and adding flour, 1 tablespoon at a time, as necessary to form a smooth dough. Place in a greased bowl, turn to coat top and sides, and cover with oiled plastic wrap. Place in warm location and let rise until doubled, 1 to 1½ hours.

❖   Gently deflate dough and turn out onto a lightly floured surface. Divide dough into 2 equal pieces. Roll each portion into a 6x10-inch rectangle. Sprinkle with minced herbs and lemon zest. Starting at the narrow end, roll dough up jelly roll style. Place seam side down into two 9x5-inch bread pans. Cover loosely with oiled plastic wrap and let rise for 40 minutes, until doubled.

❖   Bake loaves for 40 to 45 minutes in preheated oven, until light golden brown. Remove from pan and cool on racks before slicing.

FOCACCIA ROMANA
makes one large flat loaf

Bread

1	package quick rising yeast
1	cup lukewarm water (105° to 115°)
¼	cup olive oil
2	tablespoons vegetable oil
1	tablespoon sugar
½	teaspoon salt
2¾ - 3	cups unbleached flour
¼	cup corn meal

Topping

3	tablespoons olive oil
1	medium clove garlic, minced
2	teaspoons fresh rosemary leaves, crushed or 1 teaspoon dried
1-2	teaspoons Kosher salt

Rising time 1 hour 30 minutes. Preheat oven to 375°.

❖ In large bowl of an electric mixer, dissolve yeast in lukewarm water. Add olive oil, vegetable oil, sugar and salt. Mix in 1½ cups flour and beat at medium speed for about 2 minutes. The dough should leave the sides of the bowl and form a ball.

❖ Mix in remaining flour ½ cup at a time. Dough will become quite stiff. On a lightly floured surface (or with dough hook), knead dough until smooth and no longer sticky, about 10 minutes.

❖ Turn dough over in an oiled bowl to coat all sides. Cover with oiled plastic wrap and let rise until doubled in bulk, about 1 hour. Punch dough down.

❖ Oil a 13x18-inch baking sheet and sprinkle with cornmeal. Place dough in center. Using your fingers, press dough out to edges of pan. Let rise for 30 minutes.

❖ Mix oil and garlic for topping. When dough has risen, brush oil over dough lightly. Sprinkle rosemary and kosher salt on top. Bake in preheated oven for 30 minutes until crisp and golden brown.

Focaccia is wonderful with other toppings such as Parmesan cheese, sun-dried tomatoes, and olives. It also makes great pizza dough!

ENGLISH MUFFIN LOAVES
makes two loaves

Ingredients

2	cups milk
½	cup water
6	cups flour
2½	tablespoons active dry yeast
1	tablespoon sugar
2	teaspoons salt
¼	teaspoon baking soda
	shortening for greasing pans
2	tablespoons cornmeal

Rising time 45 minutes. Preheat oven to 400°.

❖ Combine milk and water in small saucepan. Heat over low heat until liquids are very warm and small bubbles start to form around edge of pan.

❖ Place 4 cups flour, yeast, sugar, salt and baking soda in food processor with metal blade inserted. Pulse a few times to blend. With the motor running, slowly pour liquids through the feed tube and mix into flour. Add remaining flour ½ cup at a time, blending well after each addition. Dough will be very sticky. (Alternately, place 4 cups flour and other dry ingredients in a large bowl. Gradually mix in liquids until a smooth sticky dough is formed. Add remaining flour ½ cup at a time and knead on a lightly floured surface for 5 to 8 minutes.)

❖ Divide dough between two 9x5-inch loaf pans which have been greased with shortening and sprinkled with cornmeal. Cover with greased plastic wrap and let rise 45 minutes.

❖ Place on middle rack in preheated oven and bake for 25 minutes, until loaves are golden brown. Cool on wire racks before slicing. Serve toasted.

QUICK HONEY WHOLE-WHEAT BREAD
makes one loaf

Ingredients

1 ½	cups unbleached flour
1	cup whole-wheat flour
½	cup wheat germ, toasted
1	tablespoon baking powder
1	teaspoon baking soda
¾	teaspoon salt
1	large egg, lightly beaten
1	cup buttermilk
⅓	cup honey
2	tablespoons butter or margarine, melted

Preheat oven to 350°.

❖ In a large bowl, combine flours, wheat germ, baking powder, baking soda and salt. In a smaller bowl, whisk together egg, buttermilk, honey and butter.

❖ Pour egg mixture into dry ingredients, mixing until just blended. Spoon into a greased 9x5-inch loaf pan. Place on middle rack in preheated oven for 50 to 55 minutes, until a toothpick inserted in center comes out clean. Cool on a wire rack for 20 minutes, remove from pan. Serve warm with soups and stews or toasted for breakfast.

To toast wheat germ, place it in a shallow baking pan and bake at 350° for 5 to 7 minutes until golden. Wheat germ is perishable and should be stored in the refrigerator.

SAILOR'S SKILLET BREAD
makes one loaf

Ingredients

½	cup sugar
1	tablespoon butter or margarine
2	cups buttermilk
½	cup raisins
2	tablespoons caraway seeds
½	teaspoon baking soda
4	cups flour
1	tablespoon baking powder
1½	teaspoons salt

Preheat oven to 350°.

❖ Beat sugar and butter together in a large mixing bowl. In another bowl, combine buttermilk, raisins, caraway seeds and baking soda. Stir into sugar mixture.

❖ Sift together flour, baking powder and salt. Gradually stir into buttermilk mixture. Turn into a greased, heavy 9-inch skillet with an oven-proof handle. (Wrap a plastic handled skillet in a double thickness of aluminum foil.)

❖ Bake in preheated oven for 60 minutes. Turn out of pan onto a clean towel and let stand 30 minutes. Cut into wedges and serve warm.

Caraway seeds and raisins give this bread a mildly sweet, anise-like flavor. Try serving it toasted for breakfast.

SOUR CHERRY ALMOND BREAD
makes one loaf

Ingredients

3	cups flour
1	cup plus 2 tablespoons sliced almonds
2	teaspoons baking powder
1	teaspoon baking soda
1	teaspoon salt
1	cup plus 1 teaspoon sugar
¼	cup butter or margarine, softened
2	large eggs, lightly beaten
1	cup buttermilk
1	teaspoon almond extract
1	cup canned, pitted sour cherries, drained and coarsely chopped

Preheat oven to 350°.

❖ In a medium bowl, combine flour, 1 cup almonds, baking powder, baking soda and salt.

❖ In a large bowl, stir together 1 cup sugar and butter. Add eggs and stir to combine well. Stir in buttermilk and almond extract. Add flour mixture, stirring just until moistened. Gently stir in cherries. Spoon into a greased 9x5 inch loaf pan. Sprinkle with remaining 2 tablespoons almonds and 1 teaspoon sugar. Press lightly into dough.

❖ Bake on middle rack in preheated oven for 60 to 70 minutes, or until a toothpick inserted in center of loaf comes out clean. Cool loaf on a rack for 10 minutes; loosen edges with a knife and turn out onto rack to cool completely.

BED & BREAKFAST SCONES
makes eight scones

Scones

2½ cups flour

¼ cup sugar

2 teaspoons baking powder

½ cup butter or margarine, well chilled

1 cup blueberries or dried fruit (raisins, cherries, cranberries)

1 large egg, plus buttermilk, to equal ¾ cup

Orange Butter

½ cup butter or margarine, softened

3 tablespoons powdered sugar

2 tablespoons orange zest, grated

Preheat oven to 425°.

❖ In a large bowl, mix flour, sugar and baking powder together until well-blended. Cut in butter, using a pastry blender or your fingers. Add fruit of your choice, distributing evenly.

❖ Mix egg and buttermilk together to equal ¾ cup and blend into flour mixture, until evenly moistened, forming a soft dough. Do not overmix.

❖ Place dough in the center of a buttered baking sheet, patting into a circle about 1-inch thick and mounded slightly higher in center. Score into eight wedges.

❖ Bake in preheated oven for 15 to 20 minutes until edges are golden brown and top is lightly golden.

❖ For Orange Butter: blend butter, powdered sugar and grated orange zest together until smooth. Serve with warm scones.

SLEEP-OVER COFFEE CAKE
serves eight to ten

Cake

2	cups flour
1	cup sugar
1	cup buttermilk
⅔	cup butter or margarine, softened
½	cup brown sugar
2	large eggs
2	tablespoons dry milk powder
1	tablespoon cinnamon
1	teaspoon baking soda
1	teaspoon baking powder
½	teaspoon salt

Topping

½	cup brown sugar
½	cup walnuts or pecans, chopped
½	teaspoon ground nutmeg
¼	cup butter or margarine, melted

Sitting time overnight. Preheat oven to 350°.

❖ Grease and flour a 9x13-inch baking pan.

❖ In large bowl of an electric mixer, combine all cake ingredients. Mix at low speed until well-blended, about 4 minutes. Place in prepared pan.

❖ Mix dry topping ingredients together and sprinkle evenly over the batter. Refrigerate overnight.

❖ The next morning, drizzle with melted butter. Place in preheated oven and bake for 30 minutes, until top is a rich golden brown. Cool for 15 minutes and serve warm.

This is a real time saver when entertaining house guests. Your guests will awaken to the aroma of freshly baked pastry. What could be more inviting!

BERRY BEST MUFFINS
makes twelve muffins

Streusel Topping

½	cup golden brown sugar, firmly packed
⅓	cup flour
1½	teaspoons lemon zest, grated
½	cup pecans or walnuts, toasted and chopped
2	tablespoons butter or margarine, softened

Muffins

1½	cups flour
¾	cup sugar
2	teaspoons baking powder
1½	teaspoons lemon zest, grated
1	teaspoon cinnamon
¼	teaspoon salt
½	cup milk
½	cup butter or margarine, melted and cooled
1	large egg
1½	cups berries (a mixture of blackberries, blueberries and raspberries)

Preheat oven to 350°.

❖ For Streusel Topping: mix brown sugar, flour and lemon zest together in bowl. Stir in nuts and butter. Mix together until butter is evenly distributed and mixture is crumbly. Set aside.

❖ For Muffins: combine flour, sugar, baking powder, lemon zest, cinnamon and salt in a large bowl. Make a well in the center. Add milk, butter and egg to the well and mix until smooth. Fold in berries.

❖ Spoon into 12 paper-lined muffin cups, filling each only ⅔ full. Top with 1 tablespoon of streusel topping. Do not overfill the muffin cups or topping will run over onto pan. Bake on middle rack in preheated oven 20 to 25 minutes, until a toothpick inserted in the center comes out clean. Place on a rack and cool 5 minutes. Remove muffins from tin and serve warm.

EGGNOG MUFFINS
makes twelve muffins

Ingredients

2	cups flour
⅔	cup sugar
1	tablespoon baking powder
½	teaspoon salt
¾	cup prepared eggnog
½	cup rum
5	tablespoons butter or margarine, melted
1	large egg, beaten
½	teaspoon nutmeg, grated

Preheat oven to 400°.

❖   Sift together flour, sugar, baking powder and salt in a large bowl. Stir in eggnog, rum, melted butter, egg and nutmeg. Spoon into 12 paper-lined muffin cups.

❖   Bake on middle rack in preheated oven for 20 minutes, until toothpick inserted in center of muffin comes out clean. Cool on rack 10 minutes before removing from pan.

Kids On The Block.
Junior League puppeteers teach healthy attitudes about people with varying abilities. This program reaches approximately 8,000 third graders in the greater Seattle schools each year.

CLOUD CAKES
serves four

Ingredients

2   cups strawberries, sliced

⅓   cup sugar

3   large eggs, separated

½   cup small curd cottage cheese

¼   cup flour

¼   teaspoon salt

⅓   cup milk

❖   Combine sliced strawberries and sugar in a small bowl. Let stand at room temperature while cooking pancakes.

❖   In a medium bowl, whisk together egg yolks and cottage cheese. Mix salt into flour and gradually whisk into egg mixture. After flour has been incorporated, gradually whisk in milk until smoothly blended. In a separate bowl which is dry and free of any oil, beat egg whites just until stiff. Gently fold into yolk-flour mixture until evenly blended. Let batter stand 5 minutes.

❖   Cook in ¼ cup portions on a hot, greased griddle. Cook until lightly browned on each side. Divide among 4 plates and serve immediately topped with sliced strawberries.

PUMPKIN PUFF PANCAKES
serves four

Ingredients

1	cup flour
2	teaspoons baking powder
1/4	teaspoon baking soda
1/8	teaspoon salt
1/8	teaspoon nutmeg
2	large eggs
2	tablespoons butter or margarine, melted
1	cup canned pumpkin puree
1/2	cup unflavored yogurt
2	tablespoons sugar
2	teaspoons lemon juice
1	teaspoon vanilla extract
	maple syrup, warmed

❖ Sift flour, baking powder, baking soda, salt and nutmeg together. Set aside.

❖ In a large bowl, whisk together eggs and melted butter. Add pumpkin, yogurt, sugar, lemon juice and vanilla. Blend in dry ingredients and mix gently until just evenly moistened.

❖ Drop by heaping tablespoonful onto hot, greased griddle. When firm and lightly browned, flip and cook other side. Serve immediately with warmed maple syrup.

TOMATO & BASIL TART
serves six

Tart Shell

1½   cups flour

½   cup butter or margarine, chilled and cut into several pieces

1   large egg

Filling

1   cup mozzarella cheese, shredded

4   Roma tomatoes, thinly sliced

¼   cup fresh basil leaves, slivered

2   tablespoons fresh chives, minced

3   large eggs

¾   cup half and half

½   teaspoon ground mustard

¼   teaspoon ground black pepper

¼   teaspoon salt

Garnish

additional fresh basil leaves for garnish

Preheat oven to 350°.

❖   For Tart Shell: combine flour and butter in processor. Process until mixture resembles fine crumbs. Add egg and process until dough holds together to form a ball. Press dough evenly over bottom and sides of a 9-inch tart pan with removable bottom. Place in preheated oven and bake for 20 minutes, until crust is firm to the touch. Remove and cool on rack. Increase oven temperature to 400°.

❖   For Filling: place mozzarella in cooled tart shell. Arrange sliced tomatoes evenly on top. Sprinkle with basil and chives.

❖   Mix together eggs, half and half, mustard, pepper and salt. Pour over mixture in tart shell. Place on a baking sheet and bake 25 minutes, until custard is firm. Remove from oven and cool on a rack 10 minutes. Remove from pan. Serve, garnished with basil leaves if desired.

SAVORY CHEDDAR PIE
serves six

Pie Shell

¾	cup flour
½	teaspoon salt
¼	teaspoon ground mustard
1	cup cheddar cheese, shredded
¼	cup butter or margarine, melted

Filling

2	cups onion, chopped
3	tablespoons butter or margarine
1	cup mushrooms, sliced
1	cup thin egg noodles, cooked and drained
2	large eggs
1	cup milk
½	teaspoon salt
½	teaspoon black pepper
1	cup cheddar cheese, shredded

Preheat oven to 350°.

❖ For Pie Shell: sift flour, salt and mustard into a medium bowl. Stir in cheddar cheese and melted butter. Mix thoroughly. Press evenly onto bottom and sides of a deep dish 9-inch pie plate.

❖ For Filling: over medium heat, sauté onion in butter until soft, about 5 minutes. Add mushrooms and cook 5 minutes more. Remove from heat and combine with noodles. Spread over crust in pan.

❖ In medium bowl, beat eggs. Add milk, salt and pepper. Pour over noodles. Sprinkle with remaining cheese.

❖ Bake in preheated oven for 35 to 40 minutes, until custard is set. Remove from oven and cool 10 minutes before serving.

This unique cheese pie is fabulous for brunch or a light supper. The cheese pastry requires no rolling and is easy to prepare.

TAKE ALONG FRITTATA
serves six

Ingredients

1	round loaf French bread, 10 to 12 inches in diameter
⅓	cup olive oil, divided
¾	pound mild Italian sausage
¾	cup onion, finely chopped
1	medium clove garlic, minced
¼	cup green pepper, diced
½	cup zucchini, diced
½	cup tomato, cored, seeded and diced
¼	cup fresh basil leaves, slivered or 1 tablespoon dried
10	large eggs
½	teaspoon salt
½	teaspoon pepper
½	cup Parmesan cheese, freshly grated

❖ Cut bread in half horizontally. Pull out soft center from each half, leaving shells about 1 inch thick. Brush inside of shells with 3 tablespoons of oil.

❖ Crumble sausage into a 10-inch skillet. Cook over moderate heat, stirring occasionally, until brown. Remove with a slotted spoon and drain on paper towels. Discard all but 2 tablespoons of drippings. Sauté onion about 5 minutes. Add garlic, green pepper, zucchini and tomato. Sauté 5 minutes more, until all liquid is evaporated. Add basil and remove from heat.

❖ In a large bowl, beat eggs with salt and pepper. Stir vegetables and sausage into egg mixture. Wipe skillet clean, add 1 tablespoon olive oil, and place over medium-low heat. When oil is hot, pour in egg mixture. Cover and cook until eggs are set, and starting to brown on bottom. Place a 12-inch plate over skillet. Invert frittata onto plate. Return pan to heat and add remaining oil. Slide frittata back into pan, topside down, and cook over medium heat until light brown. Sprinkle top with Parmesan cheese. Place bottom half of bread loaf over frittata. With one hand on bread, quickly invert pan, turning frittata out onto loaf. Place top of bread loaf over frittata. Press together firmly.

❖ Serve immediately or wrap in foil to keep warm up to 4 hours in an insulated container. When ready to serve, cut in wedges to eat by hand.

TORTE MILAN
serves six

Ingredients

1	pound fresh spinach
1	red bell pepper, chopped
2	cloves garlic, minced
1	tablespoon olive oil
¼	teaspoon ground nutmeg
⅛	teaspoon salt
	pinch black pepper
1	15-ounce container ricotta cheese
6	large eggs, beaten
1½	cups Swiss cheese, shredded
½	teaspoon salt
¼	teaspoon white pepper
1	1-pound package frozen puff pastry, thawed
1	egg white, lightly beaten
1	pound smoked ham or turkey, thinly sliced

Preheat oven to 375°.

❖ Remove stems from spinach. Wash thoroughly, drain and chop coarsely. Set aside.

❖ Over medium heat, sauté red pepper and garlic in oil until softened, about 3 minutes. Add spinach, nutmeg, salt and pepper to pan. Cook, turning frequently, until spinach is wilted, about 3 minutes. Place mixture in a dish towel and squeeze out as much liquid as possible.

❖ Combine ricotta, eggs, cheese, salt and pepper in a medium bowl.

❖ Oil an 8-inch springform pan. Place one sheet of puff pastry on a flour-dusted surface. Dust pastry with flour. Roll to a square, approximately 14 x 14 inches. Line pan with pastry, pressing gently, leaving a ½-inch overhang. Trim off corners of dough with scissors. Brush inside of pastry with some egg white. Layer filling: one third ham or turkey, half the spinach and peppers, half the cheese mixture. Repeat; top with remaining ham or turkey. Roll out remaining dough into 9-inch circle. Cut steam vent in center. Brush with some egg white. Place brushed side down over filling. Seal edge, crimping as for a pie crust. Brush top with remaining egg white. Place torte on baking sheet. Bake in preheated oven 1½ hours. Cool in pan. Remove sides. Serve at room temperature.

❖ Best if baked 6–8 hours, or overnight, in advance.

Salads

Boathouse Salad
76

Port Orchard Pear Salad
77

Ruby Salad
78

Sunset Salad
79

Meadow's Edge Salad
80

Red, White & Blueberry Salad
81

Northwest Autumn Salad
82

Spinach Salad with Warmed Shallot Vinaigrette
83

Curried Spinach Salad
84

Christmas Salad
85

Snoqualmie Salad
86

Blue Cheese Potato Salad
87

Roaring Fork Tomatoes
88

Crispy Ginger Slaw
89

Sweet & Spicy Black Bean Salad
90

Seafair Seafood Salad
91

Green Bean & Feta Salad
92

Chop Chop Salad
93

Sesame Shrimp Salad
94

Crab & Asparagus Salad
95

Seafood Caesar Salad
96

Couscous Chicken Salad
97

Beach Club Salad
98

Chicken & Two Rice Salad
99

San Juan Summer Salad
100

Grilled Chicken & Red Pepper Salad
101

BOATHOUSE SALAD
serves six

Salad

½	head red leaf lettuce
½	head Bibb lettuce
½	bunch spinach
1	Belgian endive (optional)
½	bunch watercress (optional)
½	cup pine nuts, toasted

Dressing

2	tablespoons rice or white wine vinegar
1	tablespoon mayonnaise
1	tablespoon Dijon mustard
1	teaspoon dried tarragon, crumbled
¼	teaspoon salt
¼	teaspoon white pepper
¼	teaspoon sugar
½	cup olive oil

❖ For Dressing: combine vinegar, mayonnaise, mustard, tarragon, salt, pepper and sugar in a small bowl. Slowly add oil, whisking constantly until dressing is opaque and slightly thickened.

❖ Tear salad greens into bite-sized pieces, place in a large bowl and toss with just enough dressing to coat leaves. Sprinkle salad with pine nuts and serve immediately. Any extra dressing may be refrigerated for up to 1 week.

PORT ORCHARD PEAR SALAD
serves six

Salad

¼	cup port
½	cup dried figs
1	head butter lettuce
1	head radicchio
4	pears, cored and sliced into thin wedges
¼	cup feta cheese
¼	cup walnuts, toasted and chopped

Dressing

2	tablespoons red wine vinegar
1	tablespoon lemon juice
2	teaspoons Dijon mustard
⅓	cup olive oil
	freshly ground pepper to taste

Soaking time 4 hours.

❖ For Dressing: in a small bowl, combine vinegar, lemon juice and mustard. Slowly whisk in olive oil until well-blended. Whisk in pepper. (Can be made up to 1 week ahead.) Cover and refrigerate.

❖ Warm port in a small saucepan. Add figs and let soak 4 hours or as long as overnight. Drain figs and cut into thin strips.

❖ Tear lettuce into bite-sized pieces and place on individual serving plates. Arrange pears on top and drizzle with dressing. Sprinkle feta, figs, and walnuts evenly over each plate. Serve immediately.

Dried figs can be found in most stores throughout the year. When fresh figs are available in early autumn, they are a special treat in this salad.

RUBY SALAD
serves six

Salad

1	small head radicchio
1	head red leaf lettuce
2	cups cooked beets, julienned
½	cup walnut halves, toasted
¼	cup red onion, slivered

Vinaigrette

¼	cup tarragon vinegar
¾	teaspoon dry mustard
½	teaspoon salt
½	teaspoon freshly ground pepper
½	teaspoon sugar
¾	cup walnut or olive oil
⅓	cup Roquefort cheese, crumbled

❖ For Vinaigrette: combine vine   mustard, salt, pepper and sugar in medium bowl and mix well. Slowly whisk in oil. ⌐ in Roquefort cheese.

❖ Tear lettuce into bite-sized pieces and combine with beets, walnuts and onion in a large bowl. Add vinaigrette and toss gently. Serve immediately.

Fresh beets are easy to prepare, either by baking or boiling. Be sure to leave the stem and root intact so they do not "bleed." Wrap in foil and bake at 350° 1 hour, or boil until tender. Remove skin, stem and root when cool.

SUNSET SALAD

serves six

Salad

4   cups red leaf lettuce, torn into bite-sized pieces

2   cups fresh orange sections, cut into bite-sized pieces

2   cups peeled jicama, julienned

¼   cup red onion, thinly sliced

2   tablespoons pine nuts, toasted

Dressing

¼   cup red wine vinegar

3   tablespoons cilantro leaves, chopped

1   tablespoon orange zest, grated

¾   teaspoon sugar

½   teaspoon Dijon mustard

¼   teaspoon salt

    freshly ground pepper to taste

⅓   cup canola or vegetable oil

❖ Place lettuce in a large salad b   Arrange orange, jicama and red onion on top.

❖ For Dressing: combine vinegar, cilantro, orange zest, sugar, mustard, salt and pepper in food processor or blend   With motor running, slowly add oil in a steady stream, blending until emulsified.

❖ Toss dressing with salad, sprinkle with pine nuts and serv

MEADOW'S EDGE SALAD
serves six

Salad

6	cups assorted salad greens, such as:
	spinach, arugula, watercress, endive, kale, oak leaf lettuce, or butter lettuce; torn into bite-sized pieces.

Vinaigrette

½	cup walnut oil
½	cup virgin olive oil
⅓	cup sherry vinegar
¼	cup balsamic vinegar
2	teaspoons Dijon mustard
1	medium clove garlic, minced
½	teaspoon salt
¼	teaspoon freshly ground pepper

❖ Place salad greens in a large bowl.

❖ For Vinaigrette: combine oils, vinegars, mustard, garlic, salt and pepper in a small bowl and whisk until thoroughly combined.

❖ Add dressing to greens just before serving and toss gently to coat leaves evenly.

Walnut oil is perishable and should be refrigerated to maintain freshness.

RED, WHITE & BLUEBERRY SALAD
serves six

Salad

2	heads Bibb lettuce, torn
1	head red leaf lettuce, torn
2	tablespoons small fresh mint leaves
1	cup fresh blueberries
4	ounces Brie or St. André cheese
1	thin loaf crisp French bread

Dressing

¼	cup vegetable oil
¼	cup walnut oil
2	tablespoons raspberry vinegar
2	teaspoons lemon juice, freshly squeezed
⅛	teaspoon ground nutmeg
⅛	teaspoon salt
	freshly ground pepper to taste

❖ For Dressing: in a small bowl, whisk vegetable oil, walnut oil, raspberry vinegar, lemon juice, nutmeg, salt and pepper together until well-blended.

❖ In a large bowl, toss lettuce and mint leaves with just enough dressing to coat lightly. Extra dressing may be reserved for later use. Divide greens among 6 chilled salad plates. Scatter blueberries over each salad, and arrange a thin slice of cheese in the center. Place 1 or 2 thin slices of French bread on the side of each plate. Serve immediately.

Do not wash blueberries until you are ready to use them. They do not keep as well when stored wet.

NORTHWEST AUTUMN SALAD
serves six

Salad

1	head red leaf lettuce
1	head Bibb lettuce
1	cup watercress leaves
2	Red Delicious apples
¾	cup Glazed Pecans (p. 29), chopped
¾	cup blue cheese, crumbled

Dressing

½	cup walnut or vegetable oil
¼	cup cider vinegar
2	tablespoons shallot, minced
2	tablespoons lemon juice, freshly squeezed
1	tablespoon maple syrup
¼	teaspoon salt
¼	teaspoon freshly ground pepper

❖ Tear lettuce into bite-sized pieces and place in a large salad bowl. Add watercress leaves.

❖ Cut apples into very thin wedges and place on top of greens. Sprinkle pecans and blue cheese evenly over salad.

❖ For Dressing: place oil, vinegar, shallot, lemon juice, maple sy in a small jar with a tight-fitting li⸱ ⸱⸱ke until evenly combined.

❖ Drizzle dressing over salad. Toss gently and serve immediately.

If short on time, use toasted walnuts instead of Glazed Pecans. Spread nuts on a baking sheet and bake for 10 to 12 minutes at 350°. Watch closely to avoid burning them.

SPINACH SALAD WITH WARMED SHALLOT VINAIGRETTE

serves six

Salad

2	teaspoons fresh herbs, minced (oregano, basil, rosemary, thyme)
6	ounces mild goat cheese, in log shape
2	bunches spinach, cleaned and dried
12	slices baguette

Vinaigrette

6	shallots, unpeeled
2	tablespoons olive oil
¼	cup balsamic vinegar
2	medium cloves garlic, minced
2	teaspoons Dijon mustard
½	teaspoon freshly ground pepper
½	cup extra-virgin olive oil

Preheat oven to 250°.

❖ For Vinaigrette: rub shallots with 2 tablespoons olive oil and place in a heavy baking pan. Bake in preheated ove⟨ ⟩ minutes, until shallots are very soft. Squeeze shallots from skin, dice and place in small saucepan. Add vinegar, garlic, mustard and pepper. Slowly whisk in oil. Heat to boiling, reduce heat and simmer 2 minutes. Set aside and keep warm.

❖ Place herbs on a plate and roll goat cheese in them to coat. Slice into six uniform slices.

❖ Stem spinach and tear into bite-sized pieces; place in a large bowl and toss with warm vinaigrette. (Spinach will wilt slightly.) Arrange on individual plates and garnish with sliced goat cheese and baguette. Serve immediately.

CURRIED SPINACH SALAD
serves eight

Salad

8	cups spinach leaves, cleaned and dried
2	Red Delicious apples, cored and thinly sliced
⅔	cup roasted peanuts, chopped
½	cup raisins
⅓	cup green onion, thinly sliced
2	cups shrimp, diced chicken or turkey breast (optional)

Dressing

⅔	cup vegetable oil
½	cup white wine vinegar
1	tablespoon Major Grey's chutney, finely chopped
1	teaspoon curry powder
1	teaspoon dry mustard
1	teaspoon salt
¼	teaspoon Tabasco

Standing time 2 hours.

❖ For Dressing: combine oil, vinegar, chutney, curry powder, mustard, salt and Tabasco in a jar with a tight-fitting lid. Shake well and let stand at room temperature for several hours to blend flavors.

❖ Stem spinach leaves and tear into bite-sized pieces. Place in a large salad bowl. Top with apple slices, peanuts, raisins, green onion and shrimp, chicken or turkey (if desired). Toss with dressing and serve immediately.

To clean spinach, place it in a sink full of cold water. Lift spinach out of water several times and let dirt settle to the bottom of the sink. Repeat if necessary.

CHRISTMAS SALAD
serves six

Salad

8	cups spinach leaves, cleaned and dried
1	avocado, thinly sliced
½	cup red onion, thinly sliced
1	cup pomegranate seeds
	or
½	cup dried cranberries

Dressing

4	tablespoons cranberry juice concentrate
4	tablespoons rice wine vinegar
1½	teaspoons Dijon mustard
¼	teaspoon freshly ground pepper
½	cup canola or vegetable oil

❖ Stem spinach, tear into bite-sized pieces and place in a large salad bowl. Place avocado and onion over spinach.

❖ For Dressing: combine cranberry juice concentrate, vinegar, mustard, pepper and oil in a jar with a tight-fitting lid. Shake until well-blended. Drizzle over salad.

❖ Sprinkle pomegranate seeds or dried cranberries over salad, toss gently and serve.

❖ Salad may also be served on individual plates. Toss spinach with dressing, place on plates and arrange a few slices of avocado and onion on top. Sprinkle with pomegranate seeds or dried cranberries.

Pomegranates are in season September through December.

SNOQUALMIE SALAD

serves six

Salad

1⅓	cups wild rice
3	cups water
¼	teaspoon salt
1	tart apple, cut into 1-inch chunks
½	cup red bell pepper, diced
½	cup currants
½	cup pecans, toasted and chopped
¼	cup red onion, chopped

Dressing

2	tablespoons balsamic vinegar
2	tablespoons olive oil
½	teaspoon salt
¼	teaspoon freshly ground pepper

❖ Rinse rice and place in a large epan with water and salt. Bring to a boil, reduce heat, cover and simmer until rice is just tender, about 35 minutes. (Wild rice can vary considerably in its cooking time. I ould be just tender to the bite. The water will not be completely absorbed.) Drain rice and place in a large bowl. Add apple, red pepper, currants, pecans and onion.

❖ For Dressing: whisk together vinegar, oil, salt and pepper. Pour dressing over rice mixture and stir to combine thoroughly. Serve immediately or chill up

BLUE CHEESE POTATO SALAD
serves six to eight

Salad

4	pounds small, red new potatoes, unpeeled
	lettuce leaves
½	cup blue cheese, crumbled
½	cup heavy cream
12	slices bacon, cooked crisp and crumbled
3	tablespoons chives or green onions, minced

Dressing

¼	cup cider vinegar
2	tablespoons tarragon vinegar
2	teaspoons Dijon mustard
	salt and freshly ground pepper
⅔	cup olive oil
¼	cup shallots, minced
2	tablespoons parsley, minced

❖ For Dressing: mix vinegars, m   d, salt and pepper in a small bowl. Slowly whisk in oil, then add shallots and parsley.

❖ Steam or boil potatoes until just tender. Cool slightly and cut into ¼-inch slices. Place in large bowl. Gently mix ½ cup dressing into potatoes.

❖ Line a large platter with lettuc ' aves. Place potatoes over lettuce. Whisk blue cheese and cream into remaining dressing. Spoon over potatoes. Top with crumbled bacon and chives. Serve warm or at room temperature.

Friends of Youth / Arbor House Project.
Junior League volunteers work at the Arbor House mentoring
teen mothers and conducting workshops on life skills, job planning
and parenting.

ROARING FORK TOMATOES
serves eight

Ingredients

1	15-ounce container ricotta cheese
1	medium clove garlic, blanched and minced
$\frac{1}{2}$	teaspoon salt
$\frac{1}{4}$	teaspoon white pepper
1	cup fresh basil leaves, minced
6	large, perfectly ripe tomatoes

Garnish

lettuce leaves
whole basil leaves

Chilling time overnight.

❖ Place ricotta, garlic, salt, and pepper in blender or food processor and puree. Mix in minced basil leaves. Transfer to a bowl, cover and refrigerate overnight.

❖ Line a round platter with lettuce leaves. Slice tomatoes about $\frac{1}{4}$-inch thick and place in overlapping circles around platter. Spoon ricotta mixture into center of platter. Garnish with whole fresh basil leaves.

To blanch garlic, place unpeeled cloves in a small pot of simmering water. Cook for 10 to 15 minutes. Peel and use as desired. To store, place in jar, cover with oil and refrigerate.

CRISPY GINGER SLAW
serves six to eight

Salad

2	cups Napa or green cabbage, finely shredded
1	cup carrot, shredded
1	cup snow peas, slivered
2	tablespoons cilantro (optional)

Dressing

¼	cup soy sauce
¼	cup rice vinegar
3	tablespoons Asian sesame oil
3	tablespoons vegetable oil
2	tablespoons sugar
2	tablespoons mirin
1	medium clove garlic, minced
1	tablespoon fresh ginger, minced
1	tablespoon fresh lime juice
¼	teaspoon cayenne

Chilling time overnight.

❖ For Dressing: in a small bowl, whisk together soy sauce, rice vinegar, sesame oil, vegetable oil, sugar, mirin, garlic, ginger, lime juice and cayenne. Cover and refrigerate overnight to blend flavors.

❖ In a large serving bowl, combine cabbage, carrot and snow peas. Toss to mix well. Add dressing and toss to distribute evenly. Garnish with chopped cilantro, if desired. Serve immediately.

Mirin is a sweet rice wine. It can be found in Japanese markets or in the specialty section of most supermarkets.

SWEET & SPICY BLACK BEAN SALAD
serves six

Salad

2   15-ounce cans black beans, drained and rinsed

1½   cups corn, fresh, canned or frozen, defrosted

1   cup celery, chopped

1   red bell pepper, diced

2   fresh jalapeño peppers, seeded and minced

½   cup fresh cilantro leaves, minced

Dressing

¼   cup lime juice

¼   cup canola oil

2   tablespoons brown sugar

1   tablespoon Dijon mustard

½   teaspoon salt

½   teaspoon ground pepper

Garnish

red cabbage or lettuce
several sprigs of cilantro

Chilling time 1 hour.

❖   For Dressing: combine lime juice, oil, brown sugar, mustard, salt and pepper in a jar with a tight-fitting lid. Shake until well-blended.

❖   Mix beans, corn, celery, red pepper, jalapeño and cilantro together in a shallow bowl. Pour dressing over bean mi   e and toss to coat. Cover and chill 1 hour or up to 1 day.

❖   Arrange salad in a shallow bov   ed with red cabbage or lettuce leaves. Sprinkle with cilantro leaves and serve.

Jalapeños should be seeded before using because the seeds give the pepper its heat. Remove seeds under running water and avoid touching your face.

SEAFAIR SEAFOOD SALAD
serves six

Salad

4	cups chicken stock
2	cups couscous
½	cup parsley, finely chopped
4	green onions, thinly sliced
1	red bell pepper, seeded and diced
1	green bell pepper, seeded and diced
1	yellow bell pepper, seeded and diced
½	pound tiny shrimp
½	pound crabmeat
6	large red leaf lettuce leaves

Dressing

4	plum tomatoes, halved and seeded
1	clove garlic, minced
½	cup lemon juice, freshly squeezed
½	cup fresh tarragon leaves or 3 tablespoons dried
½	teaspoon salt
1	teaspoon freshly ground pepper
½	cup olive oil

❖ In a 6-quart saucepan, bring chicken stock to a boil and gradually stir in couscous. Cover, remove from heat and allow   nd for 10 minutes, until liquid has been absorbed. Use a fork to stir and separate couscous, then spread on a baking sheet to cool.

❖ Place cooled couscous in a large bowl, with parsley, green onions and peppers. Mix thoroughly and place in refrigerator.

❖ For Dressing: in a food proce   or blender, puree tomatoes. Add garlic, lemon juice, tarragon, salt and pepper. Process 1 minute to blend. Slowly p blend until emulsified. Refrigerate until ready to use.

❖ At serving time, thoroughly mix dressing with couscous. Add seafood, toss and serve on lettuce leaves.

GREEN BEAN & FETA SALAD
serves six

Salad

1 ½ pounds fresh green beans

½ cup red onion, finely chopped

½ cup feta cheese, crumbled

½ cup walnuts, toasted and chopped

Vinaigrette

1 tablespoon lemon juice, freshly squeezed

1 tablespoon white wine vinegar

1 teaspoon Dijon mustard

¼ teaspoon dried basil, crumbled

¼ teaspoon sugar

¼ teaspoon salt

¼ teaspoon black pepper

⅓ cup olive oil

❖ Plunge beans into a large pot of rapidly boiling water. Cook five minutes, or until just tender-crisp. Meanwhile, prepare a large bowl of ice water. Drain beans and plunge into ice water until cool. Drain and pat dry with paper towels.

❖ For Vinaigrette: combine lemon juice, vinegar, mustard, basil, sugar, salt, and pepper in a small bowl. Slowly whisk in olive oil. Whisk until thickened and thoroughly blended.

❖ Place beans on a serving platter and drizzle vinaigrette over them. Top with red onion, feta and walnuts. Serve immediately or cover and chill for several hours.

Immersing cooked vegetables in ice water immediately after cooking is known as "refreshing" them. This not only stops the cooking instantly, it also sets the color.

CHOP CHOP SALAD
serves six

Salad

1	head romaine lettuce, finely chopped
4	plum tomatoes, seeded and finely chopped
1	green bell pepper, seeded and diced
1	cup each, diced: dry Italian salami, mozzarella cheese, smoked turkey breast
1	cup canned garbanzo beans, drained
$\frac{1}{2}$	cup green onions, thinly sliced

Dressing

$\frac{1}{2}$	cup red wine vinegar
2	tablespoons lemon juice, freshly squeezed
1	tablespoon Dijon mustard
3	medium cloves garlic, minced
2	teaspoons dried oregano, crumbled
1	teaspoon freshly ground pepper
$\frac{1}{2}$	teaspoon salt
$\frac{1}{2}$	teaspoon sugar
1	cup olive oil

❖ For Dressing: place vinegar, lemon juice, mustard, garlic, oregano, pepper, salt and sugar in blender or food processor with steel blade inserted. Blend for 30 seconds. Slowly drizzle in oil, blending until emulsified.

❖ Combine salad ingredients in a large bowl and toss to mix. Pour dressing over and toss again to distribute evenly. Serve immediately.

In order to maintain consistent texture, it is important to chop the salad ingredients by hand.

SESAME SHRIMP SALAD
serves six

Salad

1	tablespoon butter or margarine
1	3-ounce package ramen noodles, broken into small pieces
½	cup slivered almonds
⅓	cup sesame seeds
3	heads butter lettuce, torn into bite-sized pieces
1	cup green onion, thinly sliced
1	pound small shrimp, cooked and shelled

Dressing

½	cup rice vinegar
¼	cup vegetable oil
3	tablespoons brown sugar
1	tablespoon soy sauce
2	teaspoons Asian sesame oil

❖ Melt butter in a 10-inch skillet   medium-high heat. Add noodles and almonds. Cook, stirring often, until light golden, about 5 minutes. Add sesame seeds and stir until toasted, about 1 minute. Transfer to absorbent paper towels to cool.

❖ For Dressing: combine vineg   l, brown sugar, soy sauce and sesame oil in a small bowl. Stir to blend thoroughly.

❖ When ready to serve, set asic   cup dressing. Toss remainder with lettuce. Divide lettuce among six salad plates. Sprinkle with noodles, almonds, green onion and shrimp. Drizzle remaining dressing over salads and serve.

This also works well as a main course salad, serving four. Chive Popovers make a nice accompaniment.

CRAB & ASPARAGUS SALAD

serves six

Salad

1½	pounds fresh asparagus, trimmed
2	heads butter lettuce, washed and dried
½	cantaloupe, sliced into 12 thin wedges
¾	pound crabmeat

Dressing

3	tablespoons fresh mint leaves, minced
1	teaspoon fresh ginger, minced
⅓	cup white wine vinegar
¼	cup olive oil
1	teaspoon Dijon mustard
¼	teaspoon sugar

❖ Fill a large bowl with ice wate   et aside. In a large pan of simmering water, cook asparagus until tender, 30 seconds to 3 minutes, depending on size of asparagus. Immerse cooked asparagus in ice water until cool; drain and pat dry.

❖ For Dressing: combine mint, g....g..., vinegar, oil, mustard and sugar in a small bowl. Whisk until thoroughly combined.

❖ Divide lettuce leaves among (:s. Fan ⅙ of the asparagus and 2 melon wedges over each bed of lettuce. Top salads with crabmeat. Drizzle with dressing and serve immediately.

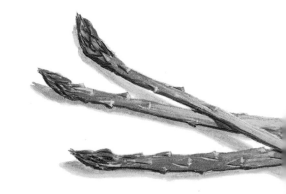

SEAFOOD CAESAR SALAD
serves six

2	medium cloves garlic
½	cup extra-virgin olive oil
1 ½	cups cubed French bread
1	pound large shrimp
1 ½	heads romaine lettuce
½	pound crab meat
⅓	cup fresh Parmesan, shredded
½	teaspoon freshly ground pepper

Dressing

3	tablespoons anchovy fillets, drained, patted dry
1	medium clove garlic
1 ½	teaspoons Dijon mustard
2	teaspoons lemon juice, freshly squeezed
2	teaspoons red wine vinegar
1 ½	teaspoons Worcestershire sauce
½	cup extra-virgin olive oil

Sitting time overnight.

❖ The night before serving, place 2 cloves garlic in a jar with ½ cup olive oil. Let stand at room temperature overnight.

❖ Discard garlic and heat olive oil in a medium skillet. Add bread cubes, turning to coat, and cook over medium heat until lightly browned, stirring often. Drain on paper towels. Set aside until ready to serve. (This may be done several days ahead. Wrap well and store in refrigerator.)

❖ In a large saucepan, bring ½ cup water to a boil. Add shrimp, cover and steam 30 seconds to 1 minute, just until pink and firm to the touch. Drain and refresh under cold running water. When shrimp are cool, shell and devein. Cover and refrigerate until ready to use.

❖ For Dressing: place anchovies, garlic and mustard in blender, or in bowl of food processor with metal blade. Process until smooth. Add lemon juice, vinegar and Worcestershire; blend for 5 seconds. With motor running, add ½ cup oil slowly and blend until thickened, about 1 minute.

❖ To Serve: tear romaine into bite-sized pieces. Place in large bowl and toss with dressing. Divide lettuce among 6 salad plates and top each serving with equal amounts of shrimp, crab and croutons. Sprinkle with Parmesan and season with pepper.

COUSCOUS CHICKEN SALAD
serves six

Salad

6	chicken breast halves, skinned
4	cups chicken stock
2	cups couscous
1	tomato, chopped
3	green onions, thinly sliced
1	15-ounce can garbanzo beans, drained
½	cup red bell pepper, diced
½	cup dried currants
¼	cup parsley, minced

Dressing

½	cup lemon juice, freshly squeezed
6	tablespoons olive oil
1	medium clove garlic, minced
¼	teaspoon cumin
¼	teaspoon curry powder
¼	teaspoon Tabasco sauce
	salt and freshly ground pepper
½	cup pine nuts, toasted

Chilling time 1 hour.

❖ Place chicken and stock in a large skillet. Simmer gently until chicken is cooked through, about 15 to 20 minutes. Remove chicken from stock. Strain stock and return to skillet.

❖ Bring stock to a boil and slowly stir in couscous. Mix thoroughly with a fork; cover and remove from heat. Let stand until stock is absorbed, about 15 minutes. Fluff couscous with a fork and spread on a baking sheet to cool. Transfer to a large bowl.

❖ Remove chicken from bone and cut into bite-sized pieces. Add to bowl with couscous. Mix in tomato, green onion, garbanzo beans, red pepper, currants and parsley.

❖ For Dressing: blend lemon juice, oil, garlic, cumin, curry powder and Tabasco in a small bowl. Season with salt and pepper to taste.

❖ Add dressing to couscous mixture and toss well. Refrigerate at least 1 hour, or up to 1 day. Sprinkle with pine nuts before serving.

BEACH CLUB SALAD
serves six

Salad

4	boneless chicken breast halves
4	cups spinach leaves, rinsed and dried
1	head romaine lettuce, washed and dried
¾	pound strawberries, hulled and sliced
1	cup blue cheese, crumbled
3	tablespoons slivered almonds, toasted

Dressing

½	cup raspberry vinegar
1	tablespoon Dijon mustard
1	medium clove garlic, minced
¼	teaspoon salt
	freshly ground pepper to taste
¾	cup canola or vegetable oil

Marinating time 4 hours or overnight. Prepare grill.

❖ Place chicken in a single layer in a non-reactive bowl.

❖ For Dressing: in a small bowl, whisk together vinegar, mustard, garlic, salt and pepper. Slowly pour in oil, whisking until emulsified. Set aside ¾ cup dressing; pour remainder over chicken breasts. Cover and chill 4 hours or overnight.

❖ Cook chicken over medium-hot coals until cooked through, 6 to 7 minutes per side. Slice across the grain into thin strips and set aside.

❖ At serving time, tear spinach and lettuce into bite-sized pieces and place in large serving bowl. Add chicken, strawberries, blue cheese and almonds. Drizzle with reserved dressing. Sprinkle with additional freshly ground pepper, if desired. Toss and serve immediately.

CHICKEN & TWO RICE SALAD
serves six

Salad

4	cups chicken stock
1	cup wild rice, uncooked
1	cup long-grain brown rice, uncooked
4	chicken breast halves, cooked and cubed
1	cup pecans, toasted
3	green onions, sliced
1/2	cup golden raisins
1/2	cup celery, chopped
2	teaspoons orange zest, grated
2	tablespoons fresh chives, minced

Orange Vinaigrette

1/4	cup rice wine vinegar
1/4	cup orange juice, freshly squeezed
2	tablespoons Dijon mustard
2	tablespoons mango chutney
1/2	teaspoon salt
1/4	teaspoon white pepper
1/2	cup canola or vegetable oil

❖ In a large saucepan, bring chicken stock to a boil. Stir in wild rice and simmer, covered, for 10 minutes. Add brown rice and simmer mixture, covered, for 30 to 35 minutes, until liquid is absorbed. Remove from heat and cool to room temperature.

❖ In a large bowl, combine rice, chicken, pecans, green onions, raisins, celery and orange zest.

❖ For Vinaigrette: combine vinegar, orange juice, mustard, chutney, salt and pepper in a small bowl. Add oil in a slow, steady stream, whisking constantly, until slightly thickened and thoroughly combined. Add to rice mixture, tossing gently to mix. Sprinkle with chives. Serve at room temperature.

To save time, use a commercially packaged blend of long-grain and wild rice.

SAN JUAN SUMMER SALAD

serves six

Salad

3	cups cooked chicken breast, cut into ½-inch pieces
3	cups cantaloupe, cut into ½-inch pieces
1	cup celery, thinly sliced
½	cup green onion, thinly sliced
⅓	cup roasted, salted cashews
	lettuce leaves

Dressing

¾	cup vegetable oil
½	cup mango chutney
¼	cup white wine vinegar
3	medium cloves garlic, minced
1	tablespoon Dijon mustard
1	tablespoon soy sauce
1	tablespoon Asian sesame oil
¾	teaspoon Tabasco sauce

❖ For Dressing: place oil, chutney, vinegar, garlic, mustard, soy sauce, sesame oil and Tabasco in processor or blender. Puree until smooth. This can be prepared 1 day ahead. Cover and refrigerate.

❖ In a large bowl, combine chicken, cantaloupe and celery. Reserve 1 tablespoon green onion and add remainder to salad. (Can be prepared 4 hours ahead. Cover and refrigerate). Before serving, add cashews to salad. Toss with enough dressing to coat. Arrange lettuce leaves on six plates. Mound salad on lettuce. Sprinkle reserved green onions on top and serve.

Cantaloupes, once ripe, should be stored in the refrigerator. These melons absorb other food odors, so wrap them in plastic.

GRILLED CHICKEN & RED PEPPER SALAD

serves six

Salad

2	red bell peppers
1 ½	pounds boneless, skinless chicken breasts
1	cucumber, peeled, seeded, thinly sliced
½	cup red onion, thinly sliced
3	tablespoons fresh cilantro, minced
1	head red leaf lettuce, shredded

Dressing

½	cup canola oil
¼	cup balsamic vinegar
¼	cup orange juice, freshly squeezed
¼	cup lime juice, freshly squeezed
3	green onions, sliced
2	medium cloves garlic, minced
¼	teaspoon salt
¼	teaspoon freshly ground pepper

Preheat oven to broil or prepare grill. Chilling time 2 hours.

❖ Halve and seed red peppers and place on an oiled, heavy baking sheet about 4 inches below broiler, skin side up, or directly on grill, skin side down. Broil until skins become completely blistered and black. Place in a plastic bag to cool. When cool enough to handle, remove skin. Cut into ½-inch strips.

❖ For Dressing: combine oil, vinegar, orange juice, lime juice, green onions, garlic, salt and pepper in a jar with a tight-fitting lid. Shake well to thoroughly combine.

❖ Cook chicken breasts under broiler or on grill for about 4 minutes on each side, until cooked through and springy to the touch.

❖ Cut chicken into strips ½-inch wide and 2 inches long. Place in a bowl with red peppers, cucumber, onion and cilantro. Add dressing and refrigerate until well chilled, at least 2 hours. Serve on individual plates on a bed of red leaf lettuce.

Cheesy Chicken & Mushroom Lasagna
104

Triple Cheese Tortellini Bake
105

Spaghetti Torta with Terrific Tomato Sauce
106

Terrific Tomato Sauce
107

Creamy Scallop Lasagna
108

Pasta with Shrimp in Tomato Cream
109

Clam Digger's Spaghetti
110

Greek Pasta Toss
111

Pasta with Grilled Chicken & Peanut Sauce
112

Stir-Fry Fettuccine
113

Red, White & Green Linguine
114

Pasta Bella
115

Garden Pasta with Spinach Pesto
116

Dilled Shrimp & Capellini Salad
117

Pacific Rim Pasta Salad
118

Tortellini Picnic Salad
119

CHEESY CHICKEN & MUSHROOM LASAGNA
serves six to eight

Ingredients

12	lasagna noodles
1	pound mushrooms, sliced
6	tablespoons butter or margarine, divided
1	tablespoon olive oil
2	medium cloves garlic, minced
$\frac{1}{3}$	cup fresh parsley, chopped
6	tablespoons flour
2	cups milk
2	cups chicken stock
$\frac{1}{2}$	teaspoon salt
$\frac{1}{4}$	teaspoon white pepper
$\frac{1}{4}$	cup half and half
3	cups cooked chicken breast, cubed
$\frac{1}{3}$	pound Prosciutto
1	15-ounce container ricotta cheese
2	cups mozzarella cheese, shredded
$\frac{1}{2}$	cup Parmesan cheese, grated

Preheat oven to 350°.

❖ Cook lasagna noodles according to package directions. Drain, rinse with cold water. Lay noodles flat on paper towels. In a large skillet, over medium-high heat, sauté mushrooms in 2 tablespoons butter and 1 tablespoon oil until golden, stirring frequently, about 5 minutes. Reduce heat to medium-low; add garlic and parsley, sauté 2 minutes more. Be careful not to brown garlic.

❖ For Sauce: in a medium saucepan, over medium heat, melt remaining 4 tablespoons butter. Add flour and cook without browning for 2 minutes, whisking constantly. Add milk and chicken stock, a little at a time. Cook until smooth and thickened, about 3 minutes, stirring constantly. To avoid scorching, remove sauce from heat as soon as it starts to boil. Sauce will not thicken any further once it has boiled. Season sauce with salt and white pepper.

❖ To Assemble: set aside 2 tablespoons Parmesan. Pour half and half in the bottom of a 10x12-inch baking pan. Lay 4 noodles in a single layer in pan. Place $\frac{1}{3}$ each of the mushroom mixture, chicken and Prosciutto over the noodle layer. Dot with $\frac{1}{3}$ of the ricotta. Sprinkle with $\frac{1}{3}$ each of the mozzarella and Parmesan. Cover with $\frac{1}{3}$ of the sauce. Repeat this process 2 more times, beginning with noodles and ending with white sauce. Sprinkle with reserved Parmesan. Bake, uncovered, until heated through, about 40 minutes. Cover and let sit 10 minutes before serving.

TRIPLE CHEESE TORTELLINI BAKE

serves four to six

Ingredients

⅓	cup dry bread crumbs
4	tablespoons butter or margarine
2	7-ounce packages dried tortellini
2	cloves garlic, minced
¼	cup shallot, minced
1	cup green pepper, chopped
1	cup red pepper, chopped
1	cup heavy cream
½	cup chicken stock
¼	cup white wine
1½	teaspoons dried basil
¼	teaspoon salt
½	teaspoon black pepper
¾	cup Gruyère, grated
¾	cup Muenster, grated
¾	cup Gouda, grated

Preheat oven to 375°.

❖ If bread crumbs are not dry, spread on a baking sheet and bake until crisp, 2 to 3 minutes. Watch carefully. In a small skillet, over medium heat, sauté bread crumbs in 2 tablespoons butter until golden. Set aside.

❖ Cook tortellini according to package directions; do not overcook. Drain, rinse with cold water, drain again. Place tortellini on an 8x11-inch baking pan.

❖ In a medium skillet, over medium heat, sauté garlic, shallot, green and red pepper until soft, about 6 minutes. Add to tortellini in baking dish. In same skillet, heat cream, chicken stock, wine, basil, salt and pepper over medium-high heat. Bring to a gentle boil and cook 5 minutes. Reduce heat to medium-low. Blend in cheeses. Stir until smooth. Do not allow to boil after cheeses have been added. Pour sauce over tortellini and stir gently to combine. Sprinkle with bread crumbs. Bake until heated through, about 30 minutes. Serve hot.

SPAGHETTI TORTA WITH TERRIFIC TOMATO SAUCE

serves six

3	tablespoons butter or margarine
3	tablespoons Parmesan cheese, grated
½	pound spaghetti
½	pound Italian sausage
1	cup onion, chopped
¼	pound mushrooms, sliced
½	cup green, pimiento-stuffed olives, sliced
2	large eggs, slightly beaten
¼	cup fresh parsley, chopped
½	teaspoon salt
½	teaspoon black pepper
1	cup fontina cheese, grated

Preheat oven to 375°.

❖   Butter an 8½-inch springform pan. Coat inside of buttered pan evenly with grated Parmesan. Cook spaghetti according to package directions. Drain, rinse with cold water, drain again. Transfer spaghetti to a large bowl.

❖   Remove sausage from casing and discard casing. Crumble sausage into a medium skillet. Sauté over medium heat until cooked through, about 10 minutes. Using a slotted spoon, transfer sausage to bowl with spaghetti. Drain all but 1 tablespoon drippings from skillet. Add onion to skillet and sauté until soft but not brown, about 5 minutes. Add mushrooms to onion and sauté until mushrooms are golden, about 7 minutes more. If skillet becomes too dry during cooking, add a tablespoon of olive oil, butter or margarine. Combine onion and mushrooms with spaghetti. Add olives, eggs, parsley, salt and pepper. Toss to combine thoroughly.

❖   Turn half the spaghetti mixture into the prepared pan, cover evenly with fontina and top with remaining spaghetti mixture. (The torta can be prepared a day ahead up to this point. Cover and refrigerate. Increase cooking time by 10 minutes if torta is chilled when placed in oven.) Cover with foil and bake 35 to 40 minutes until heated through. Remove from oven and let sit 10 minutes. Run a knife around inside edge of pan before unmolding. Cut torta into wedges with a serrated knife and serve with Terrific Tomato Sauce.

TERRIFIC TOMATO SAUCE

1	cup onion, chopped
2	tablespoons olive oil
2	medium cloves garlic, minced
1	tablespoon dried basil
2	teaspoons dried oregano
¼	teaspoon red pepper flakes
2	14-ounce cans Italian tomatoes, undrained
½	teaspoon sugar
½	teaspoon salt
½	teaspoon black pepper

❖ In a large saucepan, over medium heat, sauté onion in olive oil until soft but not brown, about 5 minutes. Add garlic, basil, oregano and red pepper flakes. Sauté 2 minutes more. In a food processor, chop tomatoes coarsely, but do not puree. Add tomatoes, sugar, salt and pepper to pan. Bring to a boil, lower heat and simmer, uncovered, for 30 minutes, stirring occasionally.

CREAMY SCALLOP LASAGNA
serves six

Ingredients

6	tablespoons butter or margarine, divided
$\frac{1}{2}$	pound mushrooms, sliced
1	cup green onion, chopped
2	cloves garlic, minced
$1\frac{1}{2}$	pounds scallops
1	teaspoon white pepper
$\frac{1}{2}$	teaspoon salt
12	spinach lasagna noodles
$\frac{1}{4}$	cup flour
1	cup chicken stock
1	cup heavy cream
$\frac{1}{3}$	cup dry white vermouth or white wine
1	teaspoon dried thyme
$\frac{1}{4}$	cup half and half
2	cups Jarlsberg cheese, shredded

Preheat oven to 350°.

❖ Melt 1 tablespoon butter in a large sauté pan over medium-high heat. Add mushrooms and sauté until golden, about 5 minutes. Reduce heat to medium. Add onion and garlic, cook 3 minutes. Transfer mushroom mixture to a bowl and set aside.

❖ Rinse scallops under cold water. Pat dry and sprinkle with pepper. Increase heat to medium-high and, in the same pan, melt 1 tablespoon butter. Sauté scallops until just opaque, 2 to 3 minutes. Do not overcook. Season with salt. Transfer to a strainer set over a bowl. Reserve drained liquid.

❖ Cook pasta according to package directions. Drain, rinse immediately with cold water and drain again.

❖ For Sauce: melt remaining butter in a medium saucepan over medium heat. Add flour and cook without browning 2 minutes, stirring constantly. Add chicken stock, cream and vermouth. Cook until smooth and thickened, about 5 minutes. Remove sauce from heat as soon as it starts to boil. Season with thyme and stir in $\frac{1}{4}$ cup of the strained scallop juices.

❖ To Assemble: pour half and half in the bottom of a 9x13-inch baking pan. Lay 4 noodles in a single layer in pan. Layer with $\frac{1}{3}$ each of the mushroom mixture, scallops and Jarlsberg. Coat with $\frac{1}{3}$ of the sauce. Repeat process twice, ending with sauce. Cover with foil. Bake 20 minutes. Remove foil and bake 20 minutes longer. Remove from oven, cover and let sit 15 minutes before serving.

PASTA WITH SHRIMP IN TOMATO CREAM
serves four to six

Ingredients

2	tablespoons olive oil
1	pound large shrimp, peeled and deveined
¼	teaspoon white pepper
¼	cup green onion, chopped
2	medium cloves garlic, minced
1	cup heavy cream
¾	cup chicken stock
½	cup vermouth
⅓	cup sun-dried tomatoes, slivered
1	tablespoon tomato paste
1	teaspoon dried basil
12	ounces linguine or spaghetti
1	cup feta cheese, crumbled
¼	cup fresh parsley, chopped

❖ Heat oil in a large skillet over medium-high heat. Sprinkle shrimp with white pepper. Sauté shrimp, green onion and garlic 2 minutes. Transfer to a separate dish, cover with foil and set aside. Reduce heat to medium. To the same pan, add cream, chicken stock, vermouth, sun-dried tomatoes, tomato paste and basil. Cook at a rolling boil until reduced and thickened, 5 to 7 minutes. Return shrimp mixture to pan. Cook 2 to 3 minutes to heat through.

❖ Meanwhile, cook pasta according to package directions. Drain well. Transfer pasta to a large serving dish. Add sauce, feta cheese and parsley. Toss well and serve immediately.

Sun-dried tomatoes can be purchased either dried or packed in oil. Bring out the flavor of the dried variety by soaking in olive oil or hot water for an hour before use.

CLAM DIGGER'S SPAGHETTI
serves four

Ingredients

2	tablespoons olive oil
½	cup onion, chopped
2	medium cloves garlic, minced
1	cup chicken stock
½	cup clam juice
½	cup white wine
¼	cup lemon juice, freshly squeezed
2	teaspoons lemon zest, grated
1	teaspoon dried oregano
3	tablespoons butter or margarine
1	tablespoon flour
½	cup Parmesan cheese, grated
1	8-ounce can chopped clams, drained
¾	pound spaghetti
1	pound fresh clams
¼	cup fresh parsley, chopped

❖ Heat olive oil in a large sauté pan over medium heat. Sauté onion until soft but not brown, about 5 minutes. Add garlic and sauté 2 minutes. Add chicken stock, clam juice, white wine, lemon juice, lemon zest and oregano. Simmer 5 minutes. Reduce heat to medium-low.

❖ In a small bowl, make a smooth paste with butter and flour. Stir this paste into the sauce. Add Parmesan cheese and canned clams. Cook until heated through, about 5 minutes. Do not allow sauce to boil after cheese has been added.

❖ Meanwhile, cook spaghetti according to package directions. While pasta is cooking, rinse fresh clams under cold water. Discard any clams that do not close when tapped. In a large, covered casserole, steam fresh clams in a few inches of water just until opened, about 5 minutes. Set aside. Discard any clams that do not open during cooking.

❖ Drain spaghetti and transfer to a large bowl. Pour sauce over pasta, add parsley and toss well. Divide pasta among individual serving dishes, top with fresh clams. Serve immediately.

GREEK PASTA TOSS
serves six to eight

Ingredients

1 1/2	pounds chicken breast, skinned and boned
1	teaspoon black pepper
1/4	cup olive oil
1/4	teaspoon salt
1/2	pound mushrooms, sliced
1	cup green onion, chopped
2	cloves garlic, minced
1	8-ounce can water-packed artichoke hearts, drained
2	cups tomato, chopped
2	teaspoons dried oregano
12	ounces corkscrew pasta
1 1/2	cups feta cheese, crumbled
1/4	cup fresh parsley, chopped

Preheat oven to warm.

❖ Cut chicken into 1-inch pieces. Sprinkle with pepper. Heat olive oil in a large skillet over medium-high heat. Add chicken and sauté until cooked through, about 3 to 4 minutes. Remove chicken from skillet with a slotted spoon and sprinkle with salt. Cover and keep warm in oven. Add mushrooms to pan. Sauté until golden, about 5 minutes. Reduce heat to medium; add green onion and garlic. Cook 2 minutes. Cut artichoke hearts into quarters. Add artichoke hearts, tomato and oregano to pan. Cook until heated through, about 5 minutes.

❖ Meanwhile, cook pasta according to package directions. Drain well.

❖ Transfer pasta to a large serving dish. Add cooked chicken, vegetable mixture and feta. Toss to thoroughly combine. Sprinkle with parsley. Serve immediately.

PASTA WITH GRILLED CHICKEN & PEANUT SAUCE
serves four to six

Sauce

1	cup chunky peanut butter
1	cup coconut milk
1/2	cup soy sauce
1/3	cup brown sugar, packed
1/4	cup dry sherry
6	dashes Tabasco sauce
3	cloves garlic, minced
1/2	teaspoon red pepper flakes
1/4	teaspoon salt

Pasta

1	small red bell pepper
1	small yellow bell pepper
1	small cucumber
1	cup asparagus pieces
1/2	cup green onion, chopped
4	chicken breasts, skinned and boned
2	teaspoons olive oil
3/4	pound spaghetti
1/4	cup peanuts, chopped
2	tablespoons fresh parsley, chopped

Preheat grill to medium-high or oven to 375°.

❖ For Sauce: in a medium saucepan, combine peanut butter, coconut milk, soy sauce, brown sugar, sherry, Tabasco, garlic, red pepper flakes and salt. Stir to combine. Cook over medium heat until smooth and heated through.

❖ For Pasta: cut red pepper, yellow pepper and cucumber into matchsticks; set aside in large bowl. Blanch asparagus in boiling water until tender, about 2 minutes. Drain, rinse immediately with cold water, drain again. Add asparagus and onion to other vegetables.

❖ Brush chicken breasts with olive oil. Grill 3 to 4 minutes per side or roast until cooked through, about 20 minutes. Brush chicken with a little peanut sauce during cooking.

❖ Meanwhile, cook spaghetti according to package directions. Drain well. Add spaghetti to vegetables, pour sauce over and toss to combine. Slice chicken breasts into thin strips. Divide pasta among individual plates. Top each serving with chicken slices, sprinkle with peanuts and parsley. Serve immediately.

STIR-FRY FETTUCCINE
serves four

Ingredients

³⁄₄	pound fettuccine
¹⁄₄	cup sesame oil
2	cups chicken breast, diced
2	teaspoons fresh ginger, minced
3	medium cloves garlic, minced
¹⁄₂	cup green onion, chopped
1	cup snow peas
3	cups broccoli florets
3	tablespoons butter or margarine
¹⁄₃	cup soy sauce
¹⁄₂	cup dry sherry
¹⁄₂	cup almonds, toasted and chopped

❖ Cook fettuccine according to package directions. Drain, rinse with cold water, drain again.

❖ Meanwhile, in a large sauté pan or wok, heat oil over medium-high heat. Add chicken and sauté 2 minutes. Add ginger, garlic, onion, snow peas and broccoli. Sauté 3 minutes more. Add butter, soy sauce and sherry. Simmer 1 minute.

❖ Add fettuccine to pan and toss to mix well. Sprinkle with almonds and serve immediately.

This one dish meal is fast and easy to make with only 2 pans to clean up afterwards... perfect after a busy day.

RED, WHITE & GREEN LINGUINE
serves six

¼	cup olive oil
1	cup green onion, chopped
1	cup red bell pepper, diced
½	cup sun-dried tomatoes, chopped
2	teaspoons dried basil
1	teaspoon dried oregano
3	cups tomato, seeded & chopped
3	medium cloves garlic, minced
¼	cup fresh parsley, minced
½	teaspoon salt
½	teaspoon black pepper
1	pound spinach linguine
¾	cup goat cheese, crumbled

❖ Heat olive oil in a large skillet over medium heat. Add green onion, red pepper, sun-dried tomatoes, basil and oregano. Sauté 5 to 6 minutes. Add tomato, garlic, parsley, salt and pepper. Cook 3 minutes more.

❖ Meanwhile, cook pasta according to package directions. Drain well.

❖ In a large serving dish, combine pasta, vegetables and goat cheese. Toss well. Serve immediately.

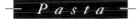

PASTA BELLA
serves four to six

Ingredients

1	cup carrots, cut into matchsticks
1	cup broccoli florets
1	cup walnuts
1	cup red bell pepper, diced
½	cup fresh parsley, chopped
⅓	cup green onion, chopped
2	medium cloves garlic, minced
1	teaspoon black pepper
¼	teaspoon salt
½	pound St. André or Brie cheese
½	pound blue cheese
1	cup olive oil
1	pound bow tie pasta

Preheat oven to 350°. Marinating time 2 to 4 hours.

❖ In a medium saucepan, blanch carrots and broccoli for 2 minutes. Drain, rinse immediately with cold water and drain on paper towels. Blot broccoli to remove as much water as possible. Toast walnuts in a single layer on a baking sheet, 8 to 10 minutes. In a large bowl, combine carrots, broccoli, walnuts, red pepper, parsley, green onion, garlic, pepper and salt. Remove rind from St. André cheese, cut into large pieces and add to bowl. Crumble blue cheese into bowl. Pour olive oil over mixture and toss gently to combine. Cover and let marinate at room temperature 2 to 4 hours.

❖ Cook pasta according to package directions; drain well. Toss pasta gently with vegetable/cheese mixture. Be careful not to overmix or cheese will melt too much. This dish is best if there are chunks of cheese throughout. Serve warm or at room temperature.

Asiago, a semi firm Italian cheese with a rich, nutty flavor, makes a great substitution for the St. André.

GARDEN PASTA WITH SPINACH PESTO
serves six

Ingredients

½	pound spinach fettuccine
½	pound egg fettuccine
2	cups broccoli florets
1	cup carrots, cut into matchsticks
1	cup frozen peas
½	cup red bell pepper, diced
½	cup Roma tomato, diced
1	cup Spinach Pesto
¼	cup Parmesan cheese, grated

Spinach Pesto

2	medium cloves garlic
2	cups packed fresh spinach leaves
¾	cup olive oil
½	cup fresh parsley
¼	cup pine nuts
2	teaspoons dried basil
½	teaspoon salt
¾	cup Parmesan cheese, grated
3	tablespoons butter or margarine, softened

❖ For Spinach Pesto: with machine running, drop garlic through feed tube of a food processor and mince. Add spinach, oil, parsley, pine nuts, basil and salt. Puree until smooth, scraping down sides a few times with rubber spatula. Transfer to a small bowl, stir in Parmesan and butter.

❖ Cook pasta according to package directions. While pasta is cooking, place all vegetables, except tomato, in a colander. When pasta is done, drain over vegetables in colander. Transfer pasta and vegetables to a large serving dish. Add tomato and pesto. Toss to combine. Place in individual serving dishes, sprinkle with grated Parmesan and serve.

❖ Note: this method results in crisp broccoli and carrots. If softer vegetables are preferred, blanch broccoli and carrots in boiling water 2 to 3 minutes first, then add them at the same time as the tomato and pesto.

DILLED SHRIMP & CAPELLINI SALAD
serves four

Salad

¾	pound capellini
1	pound medium shrimp
1	cup red bell pepper, diced
1	cup yellow bell pepper, diced
1	cup cucumber, sliced
½	cup fresh dill sprigs, chopped
¼	cup green onion, chopped

Dressing

¼	cup white wine vinegar
2	tablespoons lemon juice, freshly squeezed
1	tablespoon dry sherry
1	teaspoon honey
½	cup olive oil

❖ Cook capellini according to package directions. Drain, rinse with cold water, drain again. Peel and devein shrimp. Cook shrimp in boiling water, 1 to 2 minutes, until opaque throughout, being careful not to overcook or shrimp will become tough. Immediately rinse cooked shrimp under cold water. In a large bowl, combine capellini, shrimp, red pepper, yellow pepper, cucumber, dill and green onion.

❖ For Dressing: in a small bowl, mix together vinegar, lemon juice, sherry and honey. Add oil in a slow, steady stream, whisking constantly until thoroughly combined. Pour dressing over salad, toss to coat well and serve at room temperature.

Capellini, also known as "Angel Hair Pasta," is like very thin spaghetti. Special care must be taken not to over cook it, or it becomes mushy.

PACIFIC RIM PASTA SALAD
serves four

Salad

½	pound spaghetti
½	pound cooked shrimp
1	cup snow peas, slivered
½	cup celery, sliced
¼	cup green onion, chopped

Dressing

¼	cup honey
¼	cup lemon juice, freshly squeezed
3	tablespoons soy sauce
2	tablespoons sesame seeds
2	tablespoons fresh ginger, minced
1	medium clove garlic, minced
1	teaspoon orange zest, freshly grated
½	teaspoon red pepper flakes
¼	cup Asian sesame oil
¼	cup peanut oil

❖   For Dressing: in a medium bowl combine all ingredients except sesame and peanut oils. Add oils in a slow, steady stream, whisking constantly until well-blended and slightly thickened.

❖   Cook pasta according to package directions. Drain and rinse immediately with cold water. Drain again. Transfer pasta to a large serving dish. Add shrimp, snow peas, celery and green onion.

❖   Pour dressing over pasta mixture and toss well. Serve at room temperature.

TORTELLINI PICNIC SALAD
serves six to eight

Salad

2	12-ounce packages tortellini, fresh or frozen
1	8½-ounce can water-packed artichoke hearts, drained and quartered
1	cup tomato, diced
1	cup feta cheese, crumbled
½	cup black olives, chopped
½	cup walnuts, chopped

Dressing

¼	cup white wine vinegar
¼	cup green onion, chopped
3	medium cloves garlic, minced
1	tablespoon dried basil
1	teaspoon dried dill
½	cup olive oil

❖ Cook tortellini according to package directions. Drain. Transfer to a large bowl. Add artichoke hearts, tomato, feta, olives and walnuts. Set aside. In a small bowl, whisk together vinegar, onion, garlic, basil and dill. Add oil in a slow, steady stream, whisking constantly until thoroughly combined. Pour dressing over salad, toss to coat well and serve at room temperature.

Northwest Art
Volunteer docents take the Junior League's touring Collection of northwest Art to elementary schools throughout the greater Seattle area each year.

Seafood

Scallops with Red Pepper Sauce
122

Pacific Snapper Provencal
123

Peppered Swordfish Steaks
124

Sea Bass with Sun-dried Tomatoes & Rosemary
125

Grilled Tuna Salad
126

Pacific Rim Tuna Steaks
127

Seafood Risotto
128

Calamari Salad
129

Warm Shrimp Tarragon Salad
130

Curried Shrimp Kebobs
131

Ginger Steamed Mussels
132

Halibut with Roasted Onions & Peppers
133

Halibut with Two Butters
134

Grilled Halibut with Salsa
135

Dungeness Crab Cakes
136

HMH Blackbell '93

SCALLOPS WITH RED PEPPER SAUCE
serves six

I n g r e d i e n t s

4	red bell peppers, roasted
1	cup chicken stock
$\frac{1}{2}$	cup dry white wine
$\frac{1}{2}$	teaspoon dried basil, crumbled
1	cup butter, chilled
$1\frac{1}{2}$	pounds large scallops
2	tablespoons butter, melted
$\frac{1}{4}$	teaspoon salt
$\frac{1}{4}$	teaspoon pepper

Prepare grill.

❖   Soak 12 bamboo skewers in water for at least 30 minutes.

❖   Place roasted peppers, stock and wine in processor or blender. Puree until smooth. Pour mixture into a 12-inch skillet. Add basil and cook over medium-high heat until mixture is reduced to about $1\frac{1}{2}$ cups.

❖   Reduce heat to medium and add chilled butter a little at a time. Stir until melted and completely incorporated into sauce. Remove from heat, cover and keep warm.

❖   Drain water from skewers. Divide scallops evenly among the skewers and brush with melted butter. Place skewers on grill 2 to 4 inches above very hot coals. Cook, turning once, until scallops are opaque in the thickest part, about 3 to 5 minutes.

❖   Divide sauce among six warm dinner plates. Remove scallops from skewers and place on top of sauce. Sprinkle with salt and pepper. Serve immediately.

$1\frac{1}{2}$ cups of canned, roasted red peppers may be used to save time.

PACIFIC SNAPPER PROVENCAL
serves six

Ingredients

2	tablespoons olive oil, divided
3	medium cloves garlic, minced
3	cups plum tomatoes, chopped
1 ½	cups leeks, finely chopped
¾	cup fennel bulb, chopped
¼	teaspoon salt
¼	teaspoon pepper
¾	cup dry white wine
½	cup fish stock or clam juice
1	bay leaf
1	teaspoon dried thyme, crumbled
¼	teaspoon Tabasco sauce
6	6-ounce Pacific snapper fillets
2	tablespoons Pernod or anise-flavored liqueur
2	tablespoons fresh basil or parsley, finely chopped

❖ Heat 1 tablespoon oil in a large saucepan. Add garlic, tomatoes, leeks and fennel. Season with salt and pepper. Cook over medium heat for 3 minutes, stirring often. Add wine, stock, bay leaf, thyme and Tabasco. Bring to a boil, reduce heat and simmer 5 minutes.

❖ Heat remaining tablespoon oil in a large skillet over medium heat. Arrange snapper fillets in one layer, season with salt and pepper. Pour tomato mixture over fish. Sprinkle with Pernod, cover and simmer for about 10 minutes or until fish is opaque and flakes with a fork. Discard bay leaf. Sprinkle with fresh basil or parsley and serve immediately.

For a truly Mediterranean meal, Saffron Rice with Pine Nuts on page 211 makes a perfect side dish.

PEPPERED SWORDFISH STEAKS
serves six

2½ pounds swordfish steaks, about 1-inch thick

¼ cup whole black peppercorns, crushed

1 cup dry white wine

1 lime, thinly sliced for garnish

Lime Butter

6 tablespoons butter, softened

1 tablespoon lime juice, freshly squeezed

½ teaspoon lime zest, grated

Chilling time 2 hours. Preheat oven to broil.

❖ For Lime Butter: mix together butter, lime juice and zest until evenly combined. Place on a sheet of waxed paper and roll into a log shape. Chill at least 2 hours until firm enough to slice.

❖ Press peppercorns evenly onto top side of each swordfish steak and place in a baking pan large enough to hold them in one layer. Pour wine over fish.

❖ Broil, 4 inches from flame, until fish is opaque and flakes with a fork, about 10 minutes. Place on serving dish, top with a slice of lime butter and garnish with fresh lime slices. Serve immediately.

Other firm-fleshed fish, such as halibut or tuna, may be substituted for the swordfish in this recipe.

SEA BASS WITH SUN-DRIED TOMATOES & ROSEMARY

serves six

Ingredients

2	lemons, thinly sliced
2	pounds sea bass fillets or steaks, cut into 6 equal pieces
2	tablespoons oil reserved from sun-dried tomatoes
1	tablespoon lemon juice, freshly squeezed
2	teaspoons fresh rosemary, minced or 1 teaspoon dried
¼	teaspoon salt
¼	teaspoon pepper
¼	cup oil-packed sun-dried tomatoes
2	medium cloves garlic

Marinating time 8 hours or overnight. Preheat oven to 375°.

❖ Arrange lemon slices in the bottom of a non-reactive baking dish large enough to hold the fish in one layer. Place fish on top. Combine 1 tablespoon of oil from the tomatoes with lemon juice and brush over fish. Sprinkle fish with rosemary, salt and pepper.

❖ In a food processor or blender, mix tomatoes, remaining oil and garlic until finely chopped. Spread mixture evenly over fish. Cover and marinate in refrigerator 8 hours or overnight.

❖ Bake, uncovered, until fish is opaque in center of thickest part, about 10 minutes per inch of thickness. Serve immediately.

GRILLED TUNA SALAD
serves six

Salad

½	pound fresh green beans, trimmed
1	large fennel bulb, trimmed and cut into strips
2	bunches watercress, stems removed
1	head radicchio or red leaf lettuce
1½	pounds yellow fin tuna steaks, ¾-inch thick
24	Kalamata olives
2	tablespoons fresh chives, chopped

Dressing

1¼	cups red onion, minced
¼	cup red wine vinegar
¼	cup walnut oil
½	cup extra-virgin olive oil
¼	teaspoon salt
¼	teaspoon freshly ground pepper

Prepare grill.

❖ Bring a large pot of water to a rapid boil. Plunge beans in and cook until just tender, about 5 minutes. Meanwhile, fill a large bowl with ice water. Drain beans and refresh in ice water until cool. Drain, pat dry and set aside.

❖ Combine beans, fennel, watercress and radicchio in a large bowl.

❖ For Dressing: place red onion and vinegar in a small bowl. Slowly whisk in walnut and olive oils until incorporated. Whisk in salt and pepper.

❖ Brush 2 tablespoons dressing over tuna steaks. Grill over hot coals for 2 minutes; turn and cook to desired doneness (2 minutes for medium-rare is ideal). Cut each steak into ½-inch slices.

❖ Add remaining dressing to salad and toss. Divide among 6 plates and top with slices of tuna, dividing evenly. Place 4 olives on each plate. Sprinkle salad with chives and serve.

PACIFIC RIM TUNA STEAKS

serves six

Ingredients

6   yellow fin tuna steaks, about 4 ounces each, thick cut

Marinade

1   cup soy sauce

½   cup Asian sesame oil

½   cup lime juice

¼   cup mirin (sweet cooking sake)

2   tablespoons fresh ginger, grated

2   medium cloves garlic, minced

2   tablespoons red pepper flakes, crushed

    cilantro sprigs for garnish

Marinating time 30 minutes. Prepare grill.

❖   In a small bowl, mix together soy sauce, sesame oil, lime juice, mirin, ginger, garlic and red pepper flakes. Place tuna steaks in a non-reactive pan large enough to hold them in a single layer. Pour marinade over steaks. Cover and refrigerate 30 minutes.

❖   Lightly oil grill and light fire, allowing coals to get very hot, or set gas flame to high. Place tuna steaks on hot grill and cook 5 minutes until grill marks appear. Turn and grill 5 minutes on other side. Remove tuna from grill while it is still rare in the middle or it will become dry. Serve immediately, garnished with cilantro sprigs.

This marinade can be made ahead and stored in the refrigerator up to 2 weeks. It is also delicious with other firm, meaty fish.

SEAFOOD RISOTTO
serves six

Ingredients

6	tablespoons olive oil
½	pound medium shrimp, shelled and deveined
½	pound sea scallops, halved if large
¼	pound squid tubes, cleaned and sliced (optional)
2	medium cloves garlic, minced
½	cup tomatoes, seeded and chopped
1	cup onion, finely chopped
2	cups Arborio rice
1	cup dry white wine
4	cups chicken stock
2	cups clam juice
½	cup fresh basil leaves, slivered
½	teaspoon salt
¼	teaspoon pepper

❖ In a large, heavy skillet, heat 2 tablespoons oil over medium-high heat. Add shrimp and scallops. Sauté just until shrimp begins to color. Add squid and garlic. Sauté 2 minutes more. Seafood should be just partially cooked at this time. Add tomatoes, toss to combine and set aside.

❖ In a heavy, 6-quart saucepan, heat 4 tablespoons oil over medium-high heat and sauté onion just until softened. Add rice and stir to coat with oil. Reduce heat to medium, add wine and cook until it is absorbed. Combine chicken stock and clam juice. Add just enough to pot to cover rice. Cook, uncovered, stirring constantly, until liquid is absorbed. Continue this process of adding stock gradually as it is absorbed until all stock has been stirred into rice. This should take about 15 minutes. With last addition of stock, add seafood. Cook until all liquid is absorbed. Stir in basil. Season with salt and pepper and serve immediately.

CALAMARI SALAD
serves six

Ingredients

- ½ cup olive oil, divided
- 3 pounds squid, cleaned, patted dry and cut into rings
- 6 tablespoons lemon juice
- 1½ teaspoons lemon zest, grated
- 3 cloves garlic, minced
- 2 green onions, minced
- 1 tablespoon fennel seed, crushed
- 1 teaspoon salt
- ½ teaspoon freshly ground pepper
- 2 avocados, peeled and cut into cubes
- 3 cups fresh fennel, julienned

❖ Place ¼ cup oil in a large, heavy skillet and heat over medium-high heat. Add squid and sauté quickly, 3 to 5 minutes, stirring constantly. Do not overcook or squid will become tough.

❖ Combine lemon juice and zest in a large bowl. Slowly whisk in remaining ¼ cup oil until thoroughly blended. Stir in garlic, onions, fennel seed, salt, pepper and squid. Cover and chill until ready to serve.

❖ One hour before serving, remove salad from refrigerator. When ready to serve, add avocado and mound salad in the center of a large platter. Arrange fennel around salad in a spoke pattern. Serve immediately.

Squid, also known as calamari, has a mild, sweet flavor. Cooking time must be brief to avoid a rubbery texture.

WARM SHRIMP TARRAGON SALAD
serves six

Ingredients

3	pounds large shrimp
1/4	cup olive oil, divided
1	tomato, seeded and chopped
2/3	cup dry white wine
1/2	cup water
1/4	teaspoon salt
1/2	cup heavy cream
3	tablespoons fresh tarragon, minced
	salt and freshly ground pepper to taste
2	cups watercress leaves
2	cups arugula leaves
1	head red leaf lettuce

Dressing

1/2	cup olive oil
3	tablespoons red wine vinegar
2	tablespoons plain yogurt
1/2	teaspoon salt
1/4	teaspoon pepper
	pinch of tarragon

❖ Peel and devein shrimp, reserving shells.

❖ In a large, non-reactive skillet, heat 2 tablespoons olive oil over high heat. Add shrimp shells and cook, stirring, until they turn pink, about 1 minute. Add tomato, wine, water and salt; bring to a boil. Reduce heat to medium and cook 10 minutes. Add cream and 2 tablespoons of the tarragon; simmer 10 minutes longer.

❖ Strain sauce into a small saucepan, pressing hard on the shells; discard shells. Bring sauce to a boil over high heat. Reduce heat and simmer until sauce is reduced to about 1/3 cup and is slightly syrupy, about 10 minutes.

❖ In a large skillet, heat remaining 2 tablespoons oil over high heat. Add shrimp in 3 batches and cook each batch until opaque throughout, 3 to 5 minutes. Do not overcook or shrimp will be tough. In a large bowl, toss shrimp with the tarragon sauce and season with salt and pepper. Cover to keep warm and set aside.

❖ In a large bowl, combine watercress, arugula and red leaf lettuce.

❖ For Dressing: in a small bowl, whisk together olive oil, vinegar, yogurt, salt and pepper. Whisk in a pinch of remaining tarragon. Add dressing to greens and toss.

❖ Arrange the mixed greens on 6 plates and mound shrimp in the center. Sprinkle with remaining tablespoon of tarragon. Serve immediately.

CURRIED SHRIMP KEBOBS
serves six

Ingredients

24	large shrimp
2	tart apples
3	tablespoons lemon juice
1	tablespoon curry powder
1	tablespoon vegetable oil
¼	teaspoon salt
¼	teaspoon pepper
4	green onions, cut into 1-inch lengths

Couscous

3	cups chicken stock
1½	cups couscous
¼	cup golden raisins
½	teaspoon salt
¼	teaspoon pepper
¼	cup roasted peanuts, chopped

Preheat oven to broil or prepare grill.

❖ Peel and devein shrimp. Core and quarter apples; cut each quarter into 3/4-inch pieces. Place lemon juice, curry powder, oil, salt and pepper in a non-reactive bowl. Add shrimp and apples; toss to coat. Thread 2 shrimp, 2 pieces green onion and 2 pieces apple on each of twelve 9-inch wooden or metal skewers. (If using bamboo skewers, soak in water for 30 minutes before using so they do not burn.)

❖ For Couscous: bring chicken stock to a boil. Slowly stir in couscous, raisins, salt and pepper. Remove from heat, cover and set aside.

❖ Adjust oven rack 4 to 6 inches from heat. Broil or grill skewers, turning once, until shrimp are cooked, about 3 minutes per side.

❖ To Serve: fluff couscous with a fork, place in the center of a large serving platter. Sprinkle with peanuts. Place skewers in a spoke pattern over couscous. Serve immediately.

GINGER STEAMED MUSSELS
serves six

Ingredients

4	tablespoons Asian sesame oil
3	tablespoons fresh ginger, minced
4	medium cloves garlic, minced
4	green onions, thinly sliced
4	tablespoons soy sauce
2	cups dry white wine
1	cup chicken stock
4	pounds mussels
2	tablespoons cornstarch mixed with 1 tablespoon water
½	cup cilantro, chopped

❖ In a heavy, 8-quart pan over medium-high heat, combine sesame oil, ginger and garlic. Stir 1 minute. Remove from heat; add onion, soy sauce, wine and chicken stock.

❖ Scrub mussels under running water; pull beard free and discard. Add mussels to sauce, cover and bring to boil. Reduce heat and simmer just until mussels open, stirring often, 2 to 4 minutes. With a slotted spoon, transfer mussels from pan to serving bowl, discarding those that do not open. Cover and keep warm. Stir cornstarch mixture into cooking liquid. Bring to a boil over high heat, stirring constantly. Mix in cilantro. Pour mixture over mussels and serve immediately.

To ensure freshness, choose mussels with tightly closed shells, or those that snap shut when tapped.

HALIBUT WITH ROASTED ONIONS & PEPPERS

serves six

Ingredients

¹⁄₂	cup lime juice
¹⁄₄	cup olive oil
¹⁄₄	teaspoon white pepper
6	1-inch thick halibut steaks
3	red bell peppers, cut into ¹⁄₄-inch strips
2	Walla Walla onions, cut into ¹⁄₄-inch strips
2	tablespoons orange zest, slivered
2	tablespoons olive oil
1	clove garlic, minced
2	teaspoons fresh thyme, minced or 1 teaspoon dried
2	tablespoons lime juice, freshly squeezed
	salt and white pepper to taste

Marinating time 30 minutes. Preheat oven to 400°.

❖ Combine lime juice, ¹⁄₄ cup olive oil and white pepper in a large, non-reactive flat pan. Add halibut steaks and turn to coat both sides. Cover and marinate 30 minutes.

❖ Place red peppers, onions and orange zest in a large baking dish. Toss to coat with 2 tablespoons oil. Bake until vegetables start to brown and caramelize, stirring occasionally, about 20 minutes.

❖ Mix garlic into vegetables. Push vegetables to sides of dish. Remove fish from marinade, pat dry and place in center of baking dish. Discard marinade. Sprinkle fish with thyme. Spoon vegetables on top of fish and bake until fish is opaque in center, 10 to 12 minutes. Divide fish and vegetables among plates. Drizzle with lime juice, season with salt and pepper and serve.

HALIBUT WITH TWO BUTTERS
serves six

2 pounds halibut steaks
¼ cup lime juice
1 tablespoon oil

Hazelnut Butter

¼ **cup butter, softened**
3 **tablespoons hazelnuts, toasted and chopped**
1 **tablespoon shallot, minced**
2 **teaspoons lime zest, grated**

Ginger-Scallion Butter

¼ **cup butter, softened**
4 **scallions, thinly sliced**
1 **tablespoon fresh ginger, minced**
1 **tablespoon lemon juice, freshly squeezed**

Prepare grill.

❖ Place halibut in a single layer in a large, non-reactive pan. Combine lime juice and oil. Pour over fish, cover and refrigerate until ready to cook.

❖ For Either Butter: place ingredients in blender or food processor. Process just long enough to blend ingredients. Roll butter into log shape, wrap in plastic and chill.

❖ When ready to cook fish, place on an oiled grill, 4 to 5 inches over hot coals. After 1 minute, mark by giving it a quarter turn on the grill. Cook 2 minutes, turn over and cook about 3 minutes more, just until fish is opaque.

❖ To Serve: place individual portions of fish on serving plates and top with a slice of either Hazelnut or Ginger-Scallion Butter. Serve immediately.

These compound butters can be made up to two weeks in advance and stored in the refrigerator. They are also delicious with grilled chicken or beef. Make a double batch!

GRILLED HALIBUT WITH SALSA

serves six

2   tablespoons olive oil

2   tablespoons lime juice

¼   teaspoon Tabasco
     sauce

2   pounds fresh halibut
     fillets

Tomato Salsa

1½   cups tomato, diced

1   avocado, peeled,
     pitted and cubed

¼   cup green onion,
     thinly sliced

3   tablespoons canned
     green chiles, diced

2   tablespoons white
     wine vinegar

3   tablespoons cilantro
     leaves, minced

1   tablespoon vegetable
     oil

½   teaspoon salt

¼   teaspoon black pepper

Marinating time 2 to 4 hours. Preheat oven to broil or prepare grill.

❖   Combine olive oil, lime juice and Tabasco. Place fish fillets in a non-reactive pan large enough to hold them in 1 layer. Pour marinade over fish, cover and refrigerate 2 to 4 hours.

❖   For Tomato Salsa: combine all ingredients in a medium-sized bowl. Stir well. Cover and refrigerate 2 to 4 hours. Bring to room temperature before serving.

❖   Adjust oven rack 4 to 6 inches from heat. Place fish on grill or broiler pan and cook 10 minutes per inch of thickness, or until fish flakes easily with a fork, turning once. Serve immediately with salsa.

The Pineapple Salsa on page 137 is also delicious with this grilled halibut.

DUNGENESS CRAB CAKES
serves six

Ingredients

3	cups fresh bread crumbs, divided
2	large eggs, beaten
2	tablespoons mayonnaise
2	tablespoons each, onion, celery, red bell pepper, minced
1	tablespoon parsley, minced
1	medium clove garlic, minced
½	teaspoon salt
¼	teaspoon dried mustard
¼	teaspoon cayenne
1	pound fresh crabmeat
2	tablespoons olive oil

Chilling time 2 hours or overnight.

❖　Mix together 1 cup bread crumbs, eggs, mayonnaise, onion, celery, bell pepper, parsley, garlic and seasonings. Stir in crabmeat. Chill mixture for at least 2 hours, or up to overnight.

❖　Shape crab mixture into 12 small cakes. Evenly coat each cake with remaining bread crumbs. (You may not need to use all of the breadcrumbs.) Heat oil in a large skillet over medium heat. Cook cakes until brown and crisp, about 5 minutes per side.

❖　To Serve Crab Cakes: place a large spoonful of Orange Sauce on each plate and top with 2 crab cakes. Drizzle extra sauce over cakes. Alternately, serve hot crab cakes with Pineapple Salsa on the side.

continued on page 137

Orange Sauce

2	large shallots, minced
¼	cup white wine
1	cup orange juice, reduced by boiling to 2 tablespoons
4	tablespoons butter, cut into bits
2	tablespoons plain yogurt
2	tablespoons cream
¼	teaspoon Tabasco sauce

Pineapple Salsa

2	cups pineapple, diced
¼	cup red bell pepper, diced
¼	cup green bell pepper, diced
¼	cup red onion, diced
½	jalapeño chile, minced
2	tablespoons cilantro leaves, minced
1	tablespoon lime juice
1	tablespoon green onion, thinly sliced

❖ For Orange Sauce: in a non-reactive pan, heat shallots, wine and reduced orange juice together until the liquid is further reduced to 2 tablespoons. Gradually whisk in butter, stirring well after each addition. Remove from heat and stir in yogurt, cream and Tabasco.

❖ For Pineapple Salsa: combine all ingredients in a medium-sized bowl. Stir well, cover and refrigerate 2 to 4 hours. Bring to room temperature before serving.

Fresh cooked Dungeness crab is also delicious eaten straight from the shell. Try it with melted Ginger-Scallion Butter (page 134) for dipping.

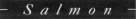

Smoked Salmon Cheesecake
140

Dill Toasts
141

Endive with Smoked Salmon & Goat Cheese
141

Smoked Salmon Quesadillas
142

Salmon Pesto Soup
143

Salmon & Salmon Chowder
144

Spring Salmon Salad
145

Salmon Bay Salad
146

Salmon with Cilantro Pesto
147

Bourbon-Basted Salmon
148

Mediterranean Salmon Bake
149

Salmon Steaks with Apricot-Horseradish Sauce
149

Salmon & Wild Rice Parchment Packages
150

Best Seattle Salmon Cakes
152

Smoked Salmon & Artichoke Fettuccine
153

Sesame-Crusted Salmon with Asian Noodles
154

Fresh Tomato & Salmon Capellini
155

Salmon & Spinach Cannelloni
156

SMOKED SALMON CHEESECAKE

serves twelve to sixteen

Ingredients

3   tablespoons butter or margarine, divided

3   tablespoons dry bread crumbs

2   tablespoons Parmesan cheese, grated

¾   cup leeks, chopped

¼   cup red bell pepper, diced

16   ounces cream cheese

2   large eggs

3   tablespoons heavy cream

¼   pound smoked salmon

¼   cup Gruyère cheese, grated

¼   teaspoon white pepper

Dill Toasts (recipe on next page) or crackers

Preheat oven to 300°.

❖   Butter an 8½ x 4½-inch loaf pan or a 9-inch round springform pan with 1 tablespoon butter. Mix together bread crumbs and Parmesan cheese. Sprinkle mixture into pan, coating all sides evenly.

❖   For Cheesecake: melt remaining butter in a medium sauté pan over medium heat. Cook leeks and red pepper until soft but not brown, about 5 minutes. Set aside. Place cream cheese, eggs and heavy cream in a food processor and blend until smooth. Transfer to a bowl and fold in sautéed leeks and red pepper, smoked salmon, Gruyère and white pepper. Combine thoroughly.

❖   Pour mixture into prepared pan. Set pan into a large baking dish. Prepare water bath by pouring hot water into baking dish until water level reaches half way up the sides of the pan. Bake, uncovered, 1 hour 40 minutes if using loaf pan, 1 hour 20 minutes if using springform pan. Turn oven off. Let sit in oven an additional hour. Cool completely.

❖   To Serve: run a knife around sides of pan. If using a loaf pan, invert pan and unmold. Slice loaf into 1-inch slices. Arrange slices on a platter like fallen dominos. If using springform pan, release sides of pan and set cheesecake on a platter. Surround with Dill Toasts or crackers. Cheesecake can be made a day in advance. Keep refrigerated. Bring to room temperature before unmolding.

DILL TOASTS
serves eight to ten

Ingredients

1	baguette
4	tablespoons butter or margarine, softened
1	tablespoon fresh dill or 1 teaspoon dried

Preheat oven to broil.

❖ Cut baguette into thin slices. Place slices in a single layer on a baking sheet. Toast slices on 1 side until light golden. Remove from oven. Blend butter and dill together.

❖ Spread the untoasted side of each slice with dill butter. Return to oven, buttered side up and broil until golden.

ENDIVE WITH SMOKED SALMON & GOAT CHEESE
makes thirty-six appetizers

Ingredients

¾	cup goat cheese
⅓	cup plain yogurt
2	tablespoons fresh dill, minced
1	tablespoon lemon juice, freshly squeezed
6	heads Belgian endive
6	ounces smoked salmon
½	cup alfalfa sprouts or watercress leaves
	freshly ground pepper

❖ Mix together goat cheese, yogurt, dill and lemon juice until smooth and spreadable.

❖ Separate endive leaves and wash quickly under cold running water. Pat dry. Slice smoked salmon into thin strips.

❖ Using a pastry bag, pipe a small rosette of cheese mixture onto each endive leaf. Tuck a tiny bunch of sprouts or watercress into side of rosette, towards the pointed end of leaf. Arrange a few strips of smoked salmon over the cheese and sprinkle with pepper. Serve chilled.

SMOKED SALMON QUESADILLAS
serves six to eight as appetizers

Ingredients

4	ounces goat cheese
3	ounces cream cheese
¼	cup sour cream
1	tablespoon red or green onion, chopped
2	teaspoons fresh dill, minced
4	8-inch flour tortillas
4	ounces smoked salmon, thinly sliced
1	tablespoon olive oil

❖ Blend goat cheese, cream cheese, sour cream, onion and dill in a small bowl. Spread cheese mixture evenly over two tortillas. Divide salmon evenly over the cheese mixture, laying pieces flat. Place remaining tortillas on top of salmon, press down gently.

❖ Brush a large, heavy skillet very lightly with olive oil, using a pastry brush or paper towel. Place pan over medium-high heat. When hot, add 1 quesadilla to pan and cook until brown spots appear on bottom tortilla, about 1 minute. Flip quesadilla and cook the other side. Transfer to a cutting board and allow to sit 1 minute. Cook remaining quesadilla. Cut quesadillas into wedges and serve immediately.

Teen Outreach Program
TOP teaches young women to be volunteers in their community and has reduced teen pregnancies and drop out rates as a result.

SALMON PESTO SOUP
serves four

Ingredients

2	tablespoons butter or margarine
1	tablespoon olive oil
1	cup leeks, chopped
½	cup red bell pepper, chopped
½	cup yellow bell pepper, chopped
5	cups chicken stock
1	cup clam juice
½	cup orzo pasta
1	pound salmon fillet
⅓	cup fresh basil, slivered
½	teaspoon salt
½	teaspoon black pepper
3	tablespoons pesto
2	tablespoons Parmesan cheese, grated

❖ Heat butter and oil in a large pot over medium heat. Sauté leeks and peppers until tender, about 4 minutes. Add chicken stock and clam juice. Bring to a simmer and add orzo. Cook until orzo is tender, about 7 minutes.

❖ Skin the salmon and remove all bones. Cut into ½-inch pieces. Add salmon and basil to pot and simmer until salmon is cooked through, about 5 minutes. Season with salt and pepper, then stir in pesto. Ladle soup into bowls. Sprinkle each serving with Parmesan cheese. Serve hot.

Use your favorite pesto for this recipe or try Spinach Pesto (page 116) for a different twist!

SALMON & SALMON CHOWDER
serves six

Ingredients

4	slices thick bacon, slivered
1	cup onion, chopped
2	medium cloves garlic, minced
5	cups chicken stock
2	cups potatoes, diced
1 ¼	cups clam juice
2	tablespoons cognac or brandy
2	small bay leaves
1	cup heavy cream
½	cup fresh parsley, chopped
¾	pound salmon, skinned, cut into 1-inch dice
½	cup smoked salmon, flaked
¼	teaspoon white pepper

❖　In a large stockpot over medium heat, cook bacon until fat is rendered, but bacon is not crisp. Remove bacon from pan with a slotted spoon. Set aside. Drain all but 2 tablespoons bacon drippings from pan. Add onion and cook until soft but not brown, about 7 minutes. Add garlic and cook 2 minutes more. Add stock, potatoes, clam juice, cognac or brandy and bay leaves. Bring to a low boil and simmer over medium heat until potatoes are tender, about 20 minutes. Add cream and parsley. Heat through. Add fresh and smoked salmon, white pepper and cooked bacon. Heat without boiling, about 5 minutes, to cook fresh salmon. Serve hot.

SPRING SALMON SALAD
serves six

Ingredients

1	cup white wine
1 ½	pounds salmon fillet
½	teaspoon salt
½	teaspoon white pepper
2	tablespoons lemon juice
12	leaves Boston lettuce
18	leaves Belgian endive
30	asparagus spears, cooked
2	tablespoons fresh dill, chopped

Dressing

½	cup heavy cream
1	tablespoon prepared horseradish
1	teaspoon Dijon mustard
1	teaspoon lemon juice, freshly squeezed
1	teaspoon red wine vinegar

❖ For Salmon: fill a large, deep sauté pan with water. Add white wine and bring to a gentle boil. Remove all bones from salmon. Season with salt and white pepper. Sprinkle with lemon juice. Wrap salmon in foil, closing edges tightly by folding several times. Place salmon package in water and poach 4 minutes. Turn package with tongs and poach 4 minutes more. Do not allow water to boil rapidly. Remove package from water and check salmon for doneness. Do not be alarmed if water has seeped into package. Cut salmon on the diagonal into 6 equal portions. Allow to cool.

❖ For Dressing: combine all dressing ingredients and whip with a wire whisk until cream is very thick and almost forming peaks.

❖ To Serve: place 2 lettuce leaves on each plate. Top with 3 endive leaves and 5 asparagus spears arranged in a fan. Lift salmon portions from foil with a spatula, leaving skin behind. Place salmon on top of salad. Spoon dressing over salmon and sprinkle with dill. Serve immediately.

All parts of this salad can be prepared up to a day in advance.

SALMON BAY SALAD
serves four

1 ½   pounds salmon fillet
       salt and black pepper

Dressing

1   medium clove garlic
1   jalapeño, stemmed and
       seeded
½   cup lime juice, freshly
       squeezed
½   cup orange juice,
       freshly squeezed
2   teaspoons Dijon
       mustard
1   teaspoon salt
¾   teaspoon ground
       cumin
¾   teaspoon sugar
½   cup olive oil

Salad

2   large bunches
       watercress
1   head romaine lettuce
½   cup fresh cilantro
       leaves
1   jicama (about 1 pound)
2   avocados

Salsa

       recipe follows

Marinating time 30 minutes. Prepare grill.

❖   For Dressing: mince garlic and jalapeño in food processor. Add remaining ingredients except oil and blend until smooth. With machine running, add oil through feed tube in a slow, steady stream. Blend until well-combined.

❖   For Salmon: remove all bones from salmon. Cut on the diagonal into 4 equal portions. Place in a shallow baking dish and spoon over ¼ cup dressing. Cover and marinate 30 minutes.

❖   For Salad: remove stems from watercress and tear romaine into bite-sized pieces. Combine with cilantro in a large bowl. Peel jicama and cut into 2-inch julienne. Add to salad and refrigerate. Cut each avocado into 8 wedges. Cover with damp paper towels and refrigerate.

❖   Drain salmon, discard marinade. Season with salt and pepper. Brush grill with vegetable oil and grill salmon, turning once, until cooked through, about 2 minutes per side.

❖   To Serve: toss salad greens with dressing and divide among 4 plates. Garnish each plate with 4 avocado wedges. Remove skin and place salmon on top of greens. Spoon salsa over salmon and avocado. Serve immediately.

continued on page 147

½	cup green onion, chopped
1	cup tomato, seeded and diced
2	fresh tomatillos, diced
½	large red bell pepper
½	large green bell pepper

❖ For Salsa: combine green onion, tomato and tomatillos. Mix in ¼ cup dressing. Set aside. Cut peppers in half lengthwise, remove seeds and flatten with palm of hand. Char skin side of peppers on grill or under broiler, until blackened, about 8 minutes. Wrap in plastic bag and steam 10 minutes. Scrape off peel. Dice peppers and add to salsa.

SALMON WITH CILANTRO PESTO
serves four

1 ½	pounds salmon fillet
2	medium cloves garlic
¼	cup walnuts
1	cup fresh cilantro leaves, packed
2	tablespoons butter or margarine
1	tablespoon olive oil
⅛	teaspoon salt
	black pepper to taste

Preheat oven to 375°.

❖ For Pesto: with machine running, drop garlic through feed tube of a food processor and mince. Add walnuts and chop finely. Add remaining ingredients, except salmon, and process into a paste.

❖ Place salmon fillet, skin side down, in a large baking dish. Remove all bones. Spread cilantro pesto evenly over salmon. Bake, uncovered, 20 to 25 minutes, or until barely opaque throughout. Do not overcook. Salmon will continue cooking for a few minutes once removed from oven. Serve hot.

BOURBON-BASTED SALMON
serves four

1 ½   pounds salmon fillet

Marinade

¼   cup brown sugar

3   tablespoons bourbon

3   tablespoons green onion, chopped

2   tablespoons soy sauce

2   tablespoons vegetable oil

Marinating time 1 hour. Prepare grill.

❖   Place salmon, skin side down, in a shallow baking dish. Remove all bones. In a small bowl, combine all marinade ingredients. Pour over salmon and marinate in refrigerator at least 1 hour.

❖   Brush the insides of a fish grilling basket with vegetable oil. Remove salmon from marinade; reserve marinade. Place salmon in basket and close securely. Grill salmon in basket over hot coals, turning once, until opaque throughout, about 7 minutes per side. Baste with reserved marinade during cooking. Serve hot or cold.

❖   Alternately, cook salmon directly on oiled grill, turning once, about 7 minutes per side.

A whole salmon fillet has a small row of bones near the top. Working with the grain of the salmon, use tweezers to pull out each bone.

MEDITERRANEAN SALMON BAKE
serves four

Ingredients

½	cup mayonnaise
⅓	cup green olives with pimiento, sliced
¼	cup fresh parsley, chopped
1	tablespoon lemon juice, freshly squeezed
1	tablespoon capers, drained
½	teaspoon Worcestershire sauce
¼	teaspoon white pepper
1½	pounds salmon fillet

Preheat oven to 375°.

❖   Combine all ingredients except salmon in a small bowl. Mix well. Lay salmon fillet, skin side down, in a large baking dish. Remove all bones. Spread olive mixture evenly over top of salmon. Bake until salmon is barely opaque throughout, 20 to 25 minutes. Do not overcook. Salmon will continue cooking for a few minutes once removed from oven. Serve hot.

SALMON STEAKS WITH APRICOT-HORSERADISH SAUCE
serves four

Ingredients

¼	cup apricot jam
4	teaspoons prepared horseradish
2	teaspoons cider vinegar
4	6-ounce salmon steaks

Preheat oven to 375°.

❖   In a small bowl, combine apricot jam, horseradish and vinegar. Spread this mixture evenly over salmon steaks. Place steaks in a shallow baking dish. Bake about 10 minutes per inch of thickness, or until meat closest to bone is barely opaque. Serve immediately.

SALMON & WILD RICE PARCHMENT PACKAGES
serves four

½ cup wild rice

1½ cups chicken stock

2 tablespoons butter or margarine

½ cup leeks, chopped

½ pound mushrooms, sliced

¼ teaspoon salt

¼ teaspoon black pepper

4 sheets parchment paper, each about 15-inches square

2 teaspoons butter, softened

4 6-ounce salmon steaks

¼ cup lemon juice, freshly squeezed

salt & black pepper to taste

Preheat oven to 350°.

❖ Place rice in a colander and rinse well. Bring stock to a boil in a medium saucepan. Add rice, reduce heat to low, cover and cook until tender, about 45 minutes. Drain rice if necessary.

❖ Melt butter in a medium sauté pan over medium-low heat. Add leeks and cook until soft but not brown, about 5 minutes. Remove leeks from pan, add to cooked rice. Increase heat to medium. Add mushrooms to same pan. Sauté until mushrooms are browned, about 8 minutes. Add mushrooms to rice mixture. Season with salt and pepper.

❖ Fold parchment paper in half and cut each piece into a semi-circle. Unfold circles. Brush inside of each piece, on one side of fold, with ½ teaspoon butter. Place salmon steaks on buttered area, next to fold. Sprinkle each steak with 1 tablespoon lemon juice. Season with salt and pepper. Place a spoonful of rice mixture in center section of each steak. Fold paper to enclose fish. Seal package by making small, overlapping folds along curved edge of paper. Be sure each fold overlaps the one before it so there are no gaps. Place packages on a baking sheet and bake, 15 to 20 minutes.

continued on page 151

Sauce

⅓	cup white wine
2	tablespoons white wine vinegar
2	tablespoons shallot, minced
8	tablespoons cold butter (not margarine)
2	teaspoons fresh dill or ½ teaspoon dried
⅛	teaspoon salt pinch of white pepper

❖ For Sauce: in a small saucepan, combine wine, vinegar and shallot over medium-high heat. Boil until reduced to 1 tablespoon, about 7 minutes. Reduce heat to low and whisk in cold butter, 1 tablespoon at a time. Allow each tablespoon to melt before adding the next one. Strain sauce through a fine sieve into another saucepan. Season with dill, salt and pepper. Just before serving, reheat sauce over medium-low heat. Do not allow sauce to boil after butter has been added.

❖ To Serve: place salmon packages on dinner plates. With scissors, cut parchment close to curved edge. Fold top back to expose salmon and rice. Spoon sauce over salmon and serve immediately.

BEST SEATTLE SALMON CAKES
serves four

Salmon Cakes

2	tablespoons butter
¼	cup green onion, sliced
1	clove garlic, minced
1	pound cooked salmon, flaked
1	cup bread crumbs
2	eggs, lightly beaten
3	tablespoons cream
¼	cup fresh basil, slivered
½	teaspoon salt
¼	teaspoon white pepper
2	tablespoons vegetable oil

Tomato-Basil Sauce

⅓	cup white wine
2	tablespoons shallot, finely chopped
1	teaspoon white wine vinegar
2	teaspoons tomato paste
2	tablespoons heavy cream
½	cup butter, chilled
¼	cup fresh basil, chopped
¼	teaspoon salt
	pinch of white pepper

Chilling time 30 minutes.

❖ For Cakes: melt butter in a small sauté pan over medium-low heat. Add green onion and cook 2 minutes. Add garlic and cook 2 minutes longer. Transfer to a medium bowl. Add salmon, bread crumbs, eggs, cream, basil, salt and pepper to bowl. Mix with a fork until well-blended. Cover and refrigerate 30 minutes.

❖ For Sauce: in a small saucepan, combine wine, shallot, vinegar and tomato paste. Bring to a boil over medium-high heat and cook until mixture is reduced to 2 tablespoons. Add cream and boil 1 minute. Reduce heat to medium and add cold butter, 1 tablespoon at a time. Whisk constantly until all butter is added and sauce has thickened. Do not allow sauce to boil again. Remove from heat and stir in basil, salt and pepper. Sauce may be reheated briefly over low heat just before serving.

❖ Form salmon mixture into 8 cakes. Heat oil in a large skillet over medium heat. Cook cakes 3 minutes per side. Divide cakes among 4 plates, spoon sauce over and serve immediately.

SMOKED SALMON & ARTICHOKE FETTUCCINE
serves four to six

Ingredients

2	tablespoons butter
2	tablespoons shallot, minced
¼	cup vermouth
2	cups heavy cream
1	13-ounce can artichoke hearts, quartered
8	ounces smoked salmon, cut into strips
1	cup tomato, seeded and chopped
¼	cup fresh parsley, chopped
1	tablespoon fresh basil or 1 teaspoon dried
½	teaspoon white pepper
½	pound egg fettuccine
½	pound spinach fettuccine
2	tablespoons olive oil

❖ Melt butter in a large saucepan over medium heat. Add shallots and cook until soft but not brown, about 3 minutes. Stir in vermouth and cook until reduced to 1 tablespoon, about 3 minutes. Add cream and cook at a rolling boil until thickened, about 6 minutes, stirring frequently. Add artichokes, salmon, tomato, parsley, basil and white pepper. Cook until heated through, about 5 minutes.

❖ Meanwhile, cook pasta according to package directions. Drain well and toss with olive oil

❖ Divide pasta among individual serving dishes, spoon sauce over and serve immediately.

To seed a tomato, cut it in half horizontally. Invert and gently squeeze each half. Use a small spoon to remove any remaining seeds.

SESAME-CRUSTED SALMON WITH ASIAN NOODLES
serves four

Ingredients

1 ½	pounds salmon fillet
1	tablespoon sesame oil
2	tablespoons sesame seeds
½	pound spaghettini
½	cup green onion, chopped
½	cup plus 2 tablespoons fresh cilantro, chopped
½	cucumber, cut into thin strips

Dressing

3	tablespoons rice wine vinegar
2	tablespoons lime juice, freshly squeezed
4	teaspoons soy sauce
1	teaspoon hot chili oil
¼	cup peanut oil
2	tablespoons Asian sesame oil

Prepare grill.

❖ Place salmon, skin side down, on a foil-lined baking sheet. Remove all bones. Make small folds in edges of foil, forming a border around salmon, until foil is just bigger than salmon. Brush salmon with 1 tablespoon sesame oil and sprinkle with sesame seeds, coating evenly. Place salmon on foil over a hot grill, close grill cover and cook 18 to 20 minutes, or until salmon is barely opaque throughout.

❖ For Dressing: in a small bowl, whisk together vinegar, lime juice, soy sauce and hot chili oil. Add peanut oil and sesame oil in a slow, steady stream, whisking constantly, until well-blended.

❖ Meanwhile, cook pasta according to package directions. Drain well. Pour dressing over pasta. Add green onion, ½ cup cilantro and cucumber. Toss to mix thoroughly. Pasta can be served hot or at room temperature.

❖ Divide pasta among individual plates. Cut salmon on the diagonal into 4 equal portions. Lift portions from foil with a spatula, leaving skin behind. Place salmon on bed of pasta and sprinkle with remaining cilantro. Serve immediately.

FRESH TOMATO & SALMON CAPELLINI
serves four

Ingredients

3	cups tomato, seeded and diced
½	cup olive oil
⅓	cup fresh basil, slivered
¼	cup shallot, finely chopped
2	tablespoons red wine vinegar
1	tablespoon fresh chives, minced
1	teaspoon lemon zest
1	teaspoon black pepper
½	teaspoon salt
	pinch of cayenne
½	cup white wine
1½	pounds salmon fillet
	salt and black pepper
1	tablespoon lemon juice
½	pound capellini
2	tablespoons olive oil

Marinating time 2 to 4 hours.

❖ For Sauce: combine first 10 ingredients in a medium bowl. Marinate at room temperature 2 to 4 hours.

❖ For Salmon: fill a large, deep sauté pan with water. Add white wine and bring to a gentle boil. Remove all bones from salmon. Season with salt and pepper to taste and sprinkle with lemon juice. Wrap salmon in aluminum foil, closing edges tightly by folding several times. Place package in water and poach 4 minutes. Turn package with tongs and poach 4 minutes longer. Do not allow water to boil rapidly. Remove package from water and check salmon for doneness. Do not be concerned if water has seeped into package. Cut salmon on the diagonal into 4 equal portions.

❖ Meanwhile, cook pasta according to package directions. Drain. Toss with olive oil.

❖ Divide pasta among 4 plates. Lift salmon portions from foil with a spatula, leaving skin behind. Place a portion on top of each bed of pasta. Spoon sauce over and serve immediately.

SALMON & SPINACH CANNELLONI
serves six

Filling

1 ½ pounds salmon fillet

2   tablespoons white wine or white vermouth

     salt & white pepper to taste

4   cups (packed) fresh spinach, washed, stems removed

2   tablespoons butter or margarine

½   cup onion, chopped

2   cloves garlic, minced

2   large eggs, lightly beaten

2   tablespoons dry bread crumbs

12   cannelloni shells

½   cup heavy cream

⅓   cup Parmesan, grated

Preheat oven to 350°.

❖ For Filling: place salmon, skin side down, in a shallow baking dish. Remove all bones. Sprinkle with wine and season with salt and pepper. Bake salmon until barely opaque throughout, about 20 to 25 minutes. When salmon is cool, remove skin and crumble by hand into a large bowl. Reduce oven temperature to 325°.

❖ Chop spinach coarsely and cook, uncovered, in a large pan with 1 inch of water, for 3 to 4 minutes, turning frequently so spinach cooks evenly. Drain thoroughly. Place cooked spinach in a towel and squeeze out as much liquid as possible. Add to salmon.

❖ Melt butter in a small sauté pan over medium heat. Add onion and sauté until soft but not brown, about 5 minutes. Add garlic and sauté 2 minutes. Add to salmon mixture. Add eggs, bread crumbs and 1 cup sauce to salmon mixture. Stir to combine well.

continued on page 157

This cannelloni can be made up to a day ahead. Store in refrigerator. Bring to room temperature for 30 minutes and bake according to instructions.

6	tablespoons butter or margarine
6	tablespoons flour
1 ½	cups whole milk
1 ½	cups chicken stock
¾	cup clam juice
¼	teaspoon salt
¼	teaspoon ground nutmeg
⅛	teaspoon white pepper
	pinch of cayenne

❖ For Sauce: melt butter in a large saucepan over medium heat. Add flour and cook without browning, whisking often, 2 minutes. Add milk, chicken stock and clam juice. Season with salt, nutmeg, white pepper and cayenne. Cook, whisking constantly, until sauce thickens. Remove from heat as soon as sauce boils. Sauce will not thicken any further once it has boiled. Hold a cold piece of butter in your fingertips and glide it slowly over the surface of the hot sauce, allowing it to melt and form a film over sauce. This will keep sauce from forming a skin. Set sauce aside.

❖ Meanwhile, cook cannelloni according to package directions. Drain, plunge into a bowl of cold water and drain again.

❖ To Assemble: coat the bottoms of two 9x13-inch baking dishes with ¼ cup each heavy cream. Using a large pastry bag without a tip, pipe filling into cannelloni shells. Place 6 filled shells into each baking dish. Spoon remaining sauce evenly over cannelloni and sprinkle with Parmesan. Cover with foil and bake 25 to 30 minutes. Uncover for last 10 minutes of baking. Serve immediately.

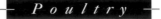

APPLE & HAZELNUT CHICKEN
serves six

Ingredients

3	pounds chicken pieces
1/2	teaspoon thyme leaves, crumbled
1/4	teaspoon salt
1/4	teaspoon pepper
4	tablespoons butter or margarine, divided
2	tablespoons vegetable oil
1	cup onion, chopped
1/4	cup applejack, brandy or Calvados
1 1/2	cups chicken stock
2	tart apples, peeled and thinly sliced
2	tablespoons sugar
1/2	cup cream
	salt and pepper to taste
1/4	cup hazelnuts, toasted and chopped

❖ Season chicken with thyme, salt and pepper. In a large sauté pan, heat 2 tablespoons butter and oil over medium-high heat. Add chicken pieces and cook until browned on all sides, about 10 minutes. Transfer chicken to a platter and cover to keep warm.

❖ Add onion to pan; cook over medium-low heat until soft and golden brown, about 20 minutes. Meanwhile, warm applejack in a small saucepan. Stand back and ignite it. When flames have subsided, pour liquid over onion. Add chicken stock and chicken; cover and simmer gently for 15 minutes. At this point chicken breasts will be done. Remove them from pan and keep warm. Continue cooking remaining chicken pieces 15 minutes longer.

❖ Meanwhile, melt remaining 2 tablespoons butter in large sauté pan. Toss apples with sugar and sauté them, stirring once or twice, until golden brown and caramelized.

❖ Arrange chicken on a platter with apples on top and alongside. Cover and keep warm.

❖ Cook stock mixture remaining in pan until reduced to a syrupy consistency. Add cream and simmer until slightly thickened. Season with salt and pepper. Drizzle sauce over chicken and apples. Sprinkle hazelnuts over top and serve immediately.

JAVA CHICKEN
serves six

6   bone-in chicken breast
     halves

Marinade

¼   cup onion, chopped

1   tablespoon vegetable
     oil

1   cup strong brewed
     coffee

¾   cup dark brown sugar

½   cup cider vinegar

1   tablespoon dry
     mustard

½   teaspoon salt

¼   teaspoon black pepper

Marinating time 8 hours.

❖   In a small saucepan, over medium heat, sauté onion in oil until transparent, about 8 minutes. Add coffee, brown sugar, vinegar, mustard, salt and pepper and bring to a boil. Reduce heat and simmer 10 minutes. Remove from heat, set aside to cool. Place chicken breasts in a single layer in a non-reactive baking pan. Pour marinade over chicken, cover and refrigerate 8 hours or overnight. Turn breasts once during marinating.

❖   Drain chicken and reserve marinade. Grill chicken over medium-hot coals on a covered grill about 20 minutes, turning once during grilling, until juices run clear when pierced with a fork. While chicken is cooking, place reserved marinade in saucepan over medium heat and bring to a boil. Reduce heat and simmer gently for 10 minutes, until thickened. Pour sauce over cooked chicken just before serving

PESTO ROAST CHICKEN
serves four

Ingredients

1   6½ to 7 pound roasting chicken

1   cup Pesto Sauce (p. 204), or purchased pesto sauce

3   tablespoons dry white wine

¾   cup plus 2 tablespoons chicken stock

2   tablespoons flour

3   tablespoons heavy cream

¼   teaspoon salt

¼   teaspoon pepper

Garnish

fresh basil

Preheat oven to 450°.

❖   Rinse chicken, pat dry. Gently loosen skin over breast and legs to form pockets. Spread pesto under skin of breast and legs, in cavity and over outer skin. Tie legs together with kitchen twine to hold shape. Tuck wings under body. Place chicken in a large roasting pan.

❖   Roast chicken in preheated oven 15 minutes. Reduce oven temperature to 375°. Roast chicken until juices run clear when chicken is pierced in thickest part of thigh, about 1 hour 15 minutes. Baste occasionally with pan juices. Remove chicken from pan and place on a platter. Cover with foil to keep warm.

❖   Pour juices from pan into a glass measuring cup and remove fat that rises to top of cup. Add wine to roasting pan and bring to a boil, scraping up any browned bits from the bottom of the pan. Add wine mixture to pan juices in measuring cup. Add enough stock to measure 1 cup and transfer mixture to a small saucepan. Combine flour with 2 tablespoons chicken stock in a small bowl. Stir until smooth. Add to saucepan and bring to a boil, stirring constantly. Boil until reduced to sauce consistency, stirring often, about 5 minutes. Reduce heat to low, whisk in cream and season with salt and pepper. Remove foil from chicken, garnish with basil and serve, passing gravy separately.

CHICKEN WITH ARTICHOKES, PEPPERS & CAPERS

serves six

Ingredients

2	tablespoons olive oil
6	boneless, skinless chicken breast halves
1	cup onion, finely chopped
1	red bell pepper, thinly sliced
2	cups mushrooms, thinly sliced
2	medium cloves garlic, minced
1/4	teaspoon each, salt, pepper, basil, oregano
1	cup each, dry white wine, chicken stock
1	cup water-packed artichoke hearts, drained and quartered
1/2	cup pitted black olives, sliced
1	tablespoon flour
1	tablespoon butter or margarine, softened
3	tablespoons capers, drained
2	tablespoons parsley, minced
3	cups cooked white or brown rice

❖ In a large skillet, heat oil over medium-high heat. Add chicken and sauté until lightly golden, about 3 minutes per side. Transfer chicken to a plate, cover and keep warm. Lower heat to medium, add onion to pan and cook 5 minutes. Add red pepper, mushrooms, garlic, salt, pepper, basil and oregano. Cook, stirring, about 2 minutes, until pepper is softened. Add wine, stock, artichoke hearts and olives. Cover and simmer 15 minutes.

❖ In a small bowl, stir flour into butter until a smooth paste is formed. Whisk butter mixture into sauce, stirring until sauce is thickened, about 3 minutes. Return chicken to pan and add capers. Simmer 10 to 12 minutes. Sprinkle with parsley and serve over rice.

Capers are tiny flower buds. Their piquant, salty flavor is good in chicken, lamb, fish and pasta dishes.

ROSEMARY WALNUT CHICKEN
serves six

¼ cup flour

½ teaspoon salt

¼ teaspoon pepper

6 boneless, skinless chicken breast halves

3 tablespoons olive oil

2 medium cloves garlic, minced

1 tablespoon dried rosemary, crumbled

1 tablespoon dried thyme, crumbled

2 cups dry white wine

2 cups chicken stock

¼ cup balsamic vinegar

½ cup feta cheese, crumbled

¼ cup green onion, thinly sliced

Herbed Walnuts

½ cup walnuts, coarsely chopped

1 tablespoon olive oil

½ teaspoon dried rosemary, crumbled

½ clove garlic, minced

¼ teaspoon salt

❖ Combine flour, salt and pepper in a shallow bowl. Dredge chicken breasts in flour mixture.

❖ In a large skillet, heat oil over medium-high heat. Add chicken and sauté until lightly browned, about 3 minutes per side. Remove chicken from pan, cover and keep warm. Reduce heat to medium. Add garlic, rosemary and thyme; cook 2 minutes more. Stir in wine, chicken stock and vinegar. Simmer, stirring occasionally, until sauce thickens, about 10 minutes. Return chicken to pan, simmer 10 to 12 minutes. Sprinkle feta cheese over chicken.

❖ Herbed Walnuts: while sauce is simmering, sauté walnuts, oil, rosemary and garlic over medium heat until the walnuts become fragrant and are lightly toasted, 3 to 4 minutes. Sprinkle with salt, drain briefly on paper towel.

❖ To Serve: place chicken on serving plates and spoon sauce over each breast. Sprinkle with green onions and Herbed Walnuts. Serve immediately.

CHICKEN WITH 40 CLOVES OF GARLIC
serves six

Ingredients

1	tablespoon olive oil
6	bone-in chicken breasts
¼	teaspoon salt
¼	teaspoon pepper
40	cloves garlic, unpeeled (about 4 heads)
1¼	cups dry white wine
¼	teaspoon dried thyme
¼	teaspoon dried rosemary
¼	cup parsley, minced
12	½-inch thick slices peasant bread

Preheat oven to 350°.

❖   Heat oil in a heavy, flameproof casserole dish wide enough to hold chicken in a single layer. Add chicken and cook over medium-high heat until evenly browned, about 10 minutes. Remove chicken from pan.

❖   Reserve 1 clove of garlic and sauté remainder over medium heat for 3 to 5 minutes, until cloves begin to turn golden. Spread cloves in a single layer and return chicken to pan. Add wine, thyme and rosemary; cover tightly.

❖   Place casserole in oven and bake 45 to 60 minutes, until cooked through. Remove casserole from oven. Sprinkle with parsley.

❖   Toast bread slices and rub both sides with the cut side of reserved garlic clove.

❖   To Serve: place 2 toasts on each plate with several cloves of garlic. Place chicken on plate, topped with sauce. Serve immediately.

Forty cloves of garlic may sound like a lot, but cooked this way the flavor is mild and does not overpower the chicken.

GRAMMY'S CHICKEN POT PIE
serves eight

Pastry

1 ¼	cups flour
½	cup butter or margarine
3	ounces cream cheese
1	large egg

Filling

1	3-pound chicken, cut into pieces
4	tablespoons butter
1	cup onion, diced
1	cup celery, diced
6	tablespoons flour
½	teaspoon salt
¼	teaspoon pepper
2 ½	cups chicken stock
1 ½	cups carrots, thinly sliced
1	10-ounce package frozen peas, defrosted
1	teaspoon dried thyme, crumbled

Chilling time 2 hours. Preheat oven to 400°.

❖ For Pastry: combine flour, butter and cream cheese in food processor. Pulse on/off several times to form coarse crumbs. Add egg and process until dough forms a ball. Wrap dough in plastic and refrigerate at least 2 hours. (Pastry dough may be made up to three days in advance and kept in the refrigerator, or it may be frozen until ready to use.)

❖ For Filling: place chicken in a large stock pot. Cover with water, bring to a boil, then lower heat to simmer. Cook until chicken is tender, about 1 hour. Remove chicken from water, cool, remove skin and bones. Cut meat into bite-sized pieces and set aside. Strain the cooking liquid, measure out 2½ cups, and discard the remainder. (Canned chicken stock may be substituted.)

❖ In a large saucepan, melt butter; add onion and celery. Sauté over medium heat for 10 minutes. Add flour, salt and pepper. Cook about 5 minutes, stirring constantly to make a roux. Slowly pour in reserved cooking liquid, stirring to make a smooth gravy. Cook until thickened, about 8 minutes. Add chicken, carrots, peas and thyme. Pour into a deep pie dish or round casserole, about 9 inches in diameter.

continued on page 167

❖ On a lightly floured board, roll pastry into a 10-inch round. Using a decorative cookie cutter, cut a shape from the center of pastry round. Lay pastry over the filling, fold edges under and crimp firmly against rim of dish. For decoration, moisten the bottom of the pastry cut-out and place it next to space from which it was cut.

❖ Place pie on a baking sheet and bake on the lowest rack of preheated oven for 45 minutes, until pastry is golden brown.

❖ Remove from oven and cool 10 minutes before serving.

This dish is great when trying to finish leftover turkey at Thanksgiving time. Substitute turkey for the chicken and use canned broth in place of the stock. Simple!

HERB GARDEN GRILLED HENS
serves six

3   Cornish game hens,
       halved, rinsed and
       patted dry

Marinade

½   cup lemon juice

¼   cup olive oil

2   tablespoons fresh
       oregano, minced

2   tablespoons fresh
       thyme, minced

2   tablespoons fresh
       rosemary, minced

4   medium cloves garlic,
       minced

¼   teaspoon salt

Marinating time overnight. Prepare grill or preheat oven to broil.

❖   In a shallow pan, mix together lemon juice, oil, oregano, thyme, rosemary, garlic and salt. Add hens, turning to coat with marinade. Cover and chill overnight.

❖   Drain hens, reserving marinade. Place on a grill over medium-hot coals and cook, basting several times with reserved marinade. Grill 20 minutes, turning once, until juices run clear when thigh is pricked with skewer. (Alternately, hens may be placed on a lightly oiled rack in the oven about 4 inches from the heat. Broil for 20 to 25 minutes, turning once.)

Place a few sprigs of fresh herbs on the grill when cooking meats and poultry. The intense aroma will add subtle flavor to the food.

NORTHWEST-OF-THE-BORDER ENCHILADAS
serves six

12   6-inch corn tortillas

Filling

1   pound chicken breasts,
     cooked and shredded

3   cups Monterey Jack
     cheese, shredded

2   tablespoons canned
     green chiles, diced

Red Chile Sauce

½   cup onion, chopped

2   cloves garlic, minced

1   tablespoon olive oil

3-4 tablespoons chili
     powder

2   tablespoons flour

1   teaspoon cumin,
     ground

1   teaspoon oregano

1   17-ounce can
     tomatoes, undrained

2   cups chicken stock

1   cup tomato sauce

Garnish

1   cup sour cream

Preheat oven to 350°.

❖ For Filling: in a medium bowl, combine chicken, 2 cups cheese, and green chiles.

❖ For Sauce: in a 10-inch skillet over medium heat, sauté onion and garlic in oil until softened, about 5 minutes. Stir in chili powder, flour, cumin and oregano. Cook 1 minute, stirring constantly. Stir in tomatoes, chicken stock and tomato sauce. Increase heat to medium-high and simmer 15 minutes. Remove from heat. Place sauce in blender or processor with metal blade and puree. Return sauce to skillet and keep warm over low heat.

❖ To Assemble: dip tortillas, one at a time, into simmering sauce. When softened, remove to a plate, allowing excess sauce to drain back into skillet. Spoon about ¼ cup filling across diameter of tortilla. Roll up tortilla and place seam side down in an oiled, shallow casserole dish. Repeat with remaining tortillas, arranging them close together in a single layer. Pour remaining sauce over enchiladas and sprinkle with remaining cheese. Cover casserole and bake in preheated oven for 15 minutes. Remove cover and bake 5 minutes more, or until heated through and lightly browned.

❖ Place two enchiladas on each serving plate. Garnish with Tomato Salsa (p.135) and sour cream. Serve immediately.

PECAN-CRUSTED CHICKEN

serves six

6   boneless, skinless
     chicken breast halves

Ingredients

1   egg yolk

2   teaspoons white wine
     vinegar

½   cup olive oil

2   tablespoons Dijon
     mustard

2   tablespoons lemon
     juice

2   medium shallots,
     chopped

½   teaspoon black pepper

¼   teaspoon Tabasco
     sauce

¾   cup pecans, finely
     chopped

¾   cup bread crumbs

Chilling time 2 hours. Preheat oven to 425°.

❖   Blend egg yolk with vinegar in the bowl of a food processor. With machine running, slowly pour olive oil through the feed tube to form a mayonnaise. Add mustard, lemon juice, shallots, pepper and Tabasco. Process, scraping bowl twice, until mixture is smooth.

❖   Combine pecans and bread crumbs on a large plate. Coat each chicken breast with mayonnaise, then dredge in breadcrumb mixture, packing crumbs onto chicken to coat well. Place on a greased baking sheet, cover and refrigerate at least 2 hours or overnight.

❖   Place chicken, uncovered, in preheated oven and immediately reduce oven temperature to 350°. Bake 25 to 30 minutes, until the crust is lightly browned and chicken is firm. Chicken may be served hot from the oven, but flavor improves when chilled before serving.

CHAMPAGNE CHICKEN
serves six

Ingredients

6	boneless, skinless chicken breast halves
6	tablespoons lemon juice, freshly squeezed
	freshly ground pepper to taste
¼	cup butter, divided
1	tablespoon olive oil
¼	cup shallots, diced
2	medium cloves garlic, minced
¾	cup chicken stock
¾	cup champagne
1¼	cups heavy cream
2	tablespoons chives, minced

❖ Pound each chicken breast to an even thickness. Sprinkle each with ½ tablespoon of lemon juice and black pepper to taste.

❖ In a large skillet, melt 2 tablespoons butter, add oil and sauté chicken over medium-high heat, about 2 minutes per side, until nicely browned. Remove from pan, cover and keep warm.

❖ In the same pan, melt remaining 2 tablespoons butter. Sauté shallots until translucent. Add garlic and cook 2 minutes more, scraping up browned bits from the bottom of the pan.

❖ Pour in chicken stock, champagne and remaining 3 tablespoons lemon juice. Bring to a boil and cook to reduce to a thin glaze. Add cream and boil for 6 minutes until thickened. Return chicken to pan and heat through. Sprinkle with minced chives and serve immediately.

Champagne Chicken is delicious on a bed of steamed white rice. For variety, try wild rice or spinach fettucine.

PROFESSOR PLUM'S CHICKEN
serves six

6	chicken breasts, boned if desired

Marinade

4	large red plums, pitted and chopped
½	cup orange juice
¼	cup soy sauce
¼	cup rice or white wine vinegar
3	tablespoons sugar
2	medium cloves garlic, minced
1	tablespoon Asian sesame oil
1	tablespoon jalapeño pepper, seeded and minced
1	tablespoon fresh ginger, minced
1	teaspoon salt
½	teaspoon dry mustard

Marinating time 4 hours or overnight. Prepare grill.

❖ For Marinade: place plums in bowl of food processor with metal blade inserted. Process until pureed. Add orange juice, soy sauce, vinegar, sugar, garlic, sesame oil, jalapeño, ginger, salt and mustard. Process until smooth. Place chicken in shallow pan and pour marinade over, reserving ¼ cup for salsa. Cover chicken and refrigerate, at least 4 hours, preferably overnight.

❖ Grill chicken over medium-hot coals until firm to the touch, about 4 minutes on each side for boneless breasts or 20 to 25 minutes for bone-in breasts.

continued on page 173

Plum Salsa

4	large red plums, pitted and diced
½	cup cilantro leaves, finely chopped
⅓	cup red onion, minced
¼	cup mint leaves, finely chopped
¼	cup reserved marinade
1	tablespoon lime juice
1	teaspoon jalapeño pepper, seeded and minced
1-2	teaspoons sugar, to taste

Garnish

lime wedges

plum wedges

❖ For Salsa: stir together plums, cilantro, onion, mint, reserved marinade, lime juice, jalapeño and sugar. Cover and refrigerate until ready to serve.

❖ To Serve: arrange chicken on a platter, garnish with lime and plum wedges. Pass salsa separately.

King County Kids' Court:
Junior League volunteers provide emotional support for child victims of abuse and prepare them for court testimony.

APRICOT ORANGE CHICKEN
serves six

6   boneless chicken breast halves, skin on

Marinade

¾   cup apricot jam

6   tablespoons orange liqueur

6   tablespoons white wine vinegar

2   tablespoons Worcestershire sauce

2   tablespoons Dijon mustard

2   tablespoons honey

½   teaspoon dried red pepper flakes

oil for brushing chicken

Marinating time overnight. Prepare grill or preheat oven to 350°.

❖   In a medium saucepan, combine jam, orange liqueur, vinegar, Worcestershire sauce, mustard, honey and red pepper flakes. Simmer, stirring, until jam and honey are melted. Cool to room temperature. In a shallow dish, marinate chicken breasts, covered and chilled, for at least 4 hours, preferably overnight. Turn the breasts several times during marinating. Remove chicken from marinade and discard marinade.

❖   Grill chicken, skin side down, over very hot coals for 4 minutes. Brush the skinless side of the chicken with oil, turn and grill 3 to 4 minutes more or until just firm to the touch.

❖   Alternately, chicken may be baked in its marinade at 350° for 40 minutes, turning after 20 minutes and basting occasionally during cooking time.

CHICKEN IN MANY MUSTARDS
serves six

6	boneless, skinless chicken breast halves

Marinade

½	cup apple juice
¼	cup Dijon mustard
¼	cup whole grain mustard
¼	cup sweet hot mustard
¼	cup white wine vinegar
¼	cup vegetable oil
2	tablespoons lemon juice
1	shallot, minced

Marinating time 8 hours. Prepare grill.

❖ Combine apple juice, mustards, vinegar, oil, lemon juice and shallot in a medium bowl and mix well.

❖ Place chicken in a single layer in a shallow pan. Pour marinade over, cover and refrigerate 8 hours or overnight.

❖ To cook, drain chicken, reserving marinade. Place chicken over medium-hot coals and grill 6 to 7 minutes per side. While chicken is grilling, place reserved marinade in a saucepan over medium heat and bring to a boil. Reduce heat and simmer 8 minutes, or until chicken has finished cooking. Spoon sauce over chicken and serve.

TURKEY & WATERCRESS SANDWICHES
serves six

Ingredients

6	pita bread rounds, sliced in half
1 ¼	pounds turkey, sliced
2	cups watercress leaves
6	plum tomatoes, thinly sliced
½	cup walnuts, chopped

Curried Apricot Mayonnaise

1 ½	cups mayonnaise
¼	cup apricot preserves
½	teaspoon curry powder

❖ For Mayonnaise: in a medium bowl, combine all ingredients, whisking to blend evenly. Cover and refrigerate until ready to use. Mayonnaise may be prepared up to 2 days ahead.

❖ For Sandwiches: spread each pita half with curried mayonnaise. Divide turkey, watercress, tomatoes and walnuts evenly between each half. Serve immediately.

For tailgating, arrange sandwich ingredients on a platter and let each person assemble their own.

TURKEY SAUTÉ WITH FRESH CRANBERRY SALSA
serves six

Ingredients

¾	teaspoon ground coriander
½	teaspoon white pepper
¼	teaspoon salt
¼	teaspoon ground ginger
2	pounds fresh turkey breast, sliced ¼-inch thick
2	tablespoons vegetable oil
½	cup orange juice
1	tablespoon lemon juice

Fresh Cranberry Salsa

¾	cup fresh pineapple, finely chopped
½	cup fresh cranberries, finely chopped
¼	cup green onion, thinly sliced
¼	cup dried dates, finely chopped
1	tablespoon honey
1	teaspoon lemon juice
1	teaspoon fresh ginger, minced
¼	teaspoon cayenne

Chilling time 1 hour.

❖ For Turkey: combine coriander, white pepper, salt and ground ginger. Sprinkle over both sides of each turkey slice.

❖ In a large skillet, heat oil over medium-high heat. Sauté turkey until lightly browned on both sides, 1 to 2 minutes per side. Add orange juice and lemon juice. Cover, reduce heat and simmer 7 to 8 minutes, just until turkey is cooked through. Serve immediately with Fresh Cranberry Salsa.

❖ For Cranberry Salsa: combine all ingredients in a small bowl. Cover and chill at least 1 hour.

This fresh cranberry salsa would enhance chicken as well as turkey. Try mixing it with cream cheese on a sandwich.

Beef Tenderloin with Five Onion Confit 180	*Madison Park Pork Medallions* 186
Peppered Herb Steaks 181	*Mustard Crumb Pork Chops* 187
Hearty Logger's Chili with Sausage 182	*Mustard & Chutney Lamb Chops* 187
Northwest Stew with Dried Cherries 183	*Lamb Stew with Orange Zest* 188
Pork Roast with Apple-Horseradish Sauce 184	*Asian Marinated Rack of Lamb* 189
Pork Roast with Spicy Pears 185	*Leg of Lamb Stuffed with Spinach & Hazelnuts* 190

BEEF TENDERLOIN WITH FIVE ONION CONFIT

serves six

Ingredients

1	3½-pound beef tenderloin
2	tablespoons vegetable oil
3	tablespoons butter or margarine
2	cups yellow onion, thinly sliced
2	cups red onion, thinly sliced
1	cup green onion, chopped
1	cup shallots, chopped
4	cloves garlic, peeled and smashed
½	cup cognac
½	cup beef stock
	salt and black pepper

Preheat oven to 400°.

❖ Trim all fat and silvery membrane from tenderloin. Tie tenderloin at 1-inch intervals with kitchen string. Heat oil in a large, heavy roasting pan. Over medium-high heat, brown tenderloin on all sides. Set meat aside on a platter. Reduce heat to medium-low and melt butter in same pan. Add onions, shallots and garlic to pan. Cook slowly until soft and golden, about 15 minutes. Add cognac and beef stock. Stir to incorporate any browned bits from bottom of pan. Set tenderloin on bed of onions. Cover with foil and place in oven. Cook beef about 25 minutes, or until an instant-read thermometer reads 115° for medium-rare.

❖ Remove tenderloin from roasting pan and let sit, tented with foil, for 10 minutes before carving. Return roasting pan to top of stove. Cook onion confit over medium heat until liquid is evaporated and confit is thickened and golden. Season with salt and black pepper to taste.

❖ To Serve: remove string and slice tenderloin into ½-inch slices. Serve immediately with onion confit on the side.

PEPPERED HERB STEAKS
serves six

2   flank steaks, each
approximately 2
pounds

Marinade

¾   cup olive oil

⅓   cup red wine vinegar

¼   cup Dijon mustard

4   large cloves garlic,
minced

4   tablespoons green
onion, chopped

1   tablespoon + 1
teaspoon black pepper,
coarsely ground

1   tablespoon fresh
thyme, minced or 1
teaspoon dried

1   tablespoon fresh
rosemary, minced or 1
teaspoon dried

1   teaspoon salt

Garnish

   fresh thyme or
rosemary sprigs
(optional)

Marinating time up to 24 hours. Prepare grill.

❖   Whisk together first 9 ingredients in a small bowl. Place steaks in a single layer in a large baking dish. Pour marinade over and turn steaks to coat. Cover and refrigerate several hours or overnight. Bring to room temperature before cooking.

❖   Grill steaks over medium-hot coals about 5 minutes per side for medium-rare, 7 minutes per side for medium. Thinly slice steaks diagonally across the grain. Garnish with thyme or rosemary sprigs, if desired, and serve.

Flank steak tends to be less tender than other beef cuts and should be marinated for several hours before cooking.

HEARTY LOGGER'S CHILI WITH SAUSAGE
serves six

Ingredients

1	pound lean ground beef
1	pound Kielbasa sausage
1	tablespoon olive oil
1	cup onion, chopped
1	cup green pepper, diced
2	cloves garlic, minced
1	16-ounce can kidney beans, drained
1	16-ounce can stewed tomatoes, undrained
1	16-ounce can tomato sauce
2	bay leaves
1	teaspoon salt
1	teaspoon chili powder
1	teaspoon dried oregano
$\frac{1}{3}$	teaspoon white pepper
$\frac{1}{3}$	teaspoon black pepper
$\frac{1}{8}$	teaspoon cayenne

Garnish

sour cream and/or shredded cheddar cheese (optional)

❖ Sauté ground beef in a large, heavy skillet, drain and set aside in separate dish. Cut sausage into ½-inch slices then cut each slice in half. In the same pan, sauté sausage until lightly browned; set aside with the ground beef. In the same pan, sauté onions and green pepper in olive oil over medium heat until soft but not brown. Add garlic and sauté 2 minutes more. Add ground beef and sausage back into pan together with remaining ingredients. Simmer, uncovered, for 1 hour. Serve with a garnish of sour cream and/or grated cheddar cheese, if desired.

NORTHWEST STEW WITH DRIED CHERRIES
serves six

Ingredients

2½   pounds beef chuck, boneless

3   tablespoons flour

1¼   teaspoons salt

½   teaspoon allspice

½   teaspoon cinnamon

½   teaspoon black pepper

4   tablespoons vegetable oil

3   cups onion, thinly sliced

1   cup dried sour cherries, pitted

2   tablespoons sugar

2   tablespoons red wine vinegar

2   tablespoons water

1   cup dry red wine

1   cup beef stock

½   pound mushrooms, quartered

Preheat oven to 350°.

❖   Cut beef into 1-inch cubes. Combine flour, salt, allspice, cinnamon and pepper in a plastic bag. Add beef to bag and shake, coating pieces evenly. Heat 1 tablespoon oil in a large, heavy skillet over medium-high heat. Add ⅓ of the beef and cook until browned on all sides, stirring frequently, about 5 minutes. Transfer meat to a heavy, medium Dutch oven. Repeat with remaining meat in 2 batches, adding 1 tablespoon oil to skillet for each batch. Transfer meat to Dutch oven as it browns.

❖   Reduce heat to medium. Add remaining tablespoon oil to same skillet. Add onions and cherries. Cook until onions are soft and light brown, about 10 minutes. Stir frequently, scraping up all browned bits from meat and incorporating into onions. Mix in sugar, vinegar and water. Increase heat to medium-high and cook until onions brown, stirring frequently, about 5 minutes

❖   Add onion mixture to beef in Dutch oven. Mix in wine, stock and mushrooms. Cover and bake until beef is tender, about 2 hours. Uncover stew during last 30 minutes of baking if liquid is too thin. Add a small amount of beef stock or red wine if stew is too dry.

❖   Can be prepared 2 days in advance. Cover and refrigerate. Rewarm over low heat.

PORK ROAST WITH APPLE-HORSERADISH SAUCE
serves six

1   5-pound pork loin
     roast

Marinade

½   cup dry sherry

¼   cup soy sauce

2   tablespoons Dijon
     mustard

2   tablespoons ground
     ginger

3   medium cloves garlic,
     minced

1   teaspoon dried thyme

½   teaspoon white pepper

Glaze

1   cup apple jelly

3   tablespoons lemon
     juice, freshly squeezed

2   tablespoons dry sherry

2   tablespoons soy sauce

Sauce

2   cups chunky apple
     sauce

3   tablespoons prepared
     horseradish

2   tablespoons lemon
     juice, freshly squeezed

Marinating time up to 24 hours. Preheat oven to 325°.

❖   To Marinate and Cook: mix together all marinade ingredients and pour over roast. Marinate at least 2 hours or overnight in refrigerator, turning occasionally. Drain marinade off meat and reserve. Place meat in a roasting pan and cover with a loose tent of aluminum foil. Roast until an instant-read thermometer registers 150° to 160° when inserted in center of roast, about 3 hours. Baste roast with glaze every 15 minutes for last 2 hours of cooking.

❖   For Glaze: in a medium saucepan, mix together all glaze ingredients and add reserved meat marinade. Bring to a boil, reduce heat and simmer 10 minutes. Reserve 1 cup of glaze to reheat and spoon over meat when serving. Use remaining glaze to baste roast.

❖   For Sauce: in a small bowl, mix together all sauce ingredients. Serve warm or chilled.

❖   To Serve: carve roast into ½-inch slices. Serve 2 slices per person; spoon 2 to 3 tablespoons warm glaze over each serving. Serve Apple-Horseradish Sauce on the side.

PORK ROAST WITH SPICY PEARS
serves four

Ingredients

1	3-pound pork loin roast
2	medium cloves garlic, sliced
1	tablespoon fresh rosemary or 1 teaspoon dried
	freshly ground black pepper
2	tablespoons butter or margarine
4	cups pears, peeled and diced
1	clove garlic, minced
1/4	cup dry red wine
3	tablespoons red currant jelly
2	tablespoons soy sauce
2	teaspoons red wine vinegar
	pinch of cayenne
	salt to taste

Preheat oven to 400°.

❖ With a small, pointed knife, make several small slits in surface of pork roast. Insert garlic slices into the slits. Pat pork all over with rosemary and black pepper. Place in a dry, heavy roasting pan. Roast pork, uncovered, about 1 hour, or until an instant-read thermometer reads 140°.

❖ Meanwhile, melt butter in a large sauté pan over medium heat. Add pears and minced garlic. Cover and cook, stirring occasionally, until pears are tender, 5 to 10 minutes, depending on ripeness of pears. Be careful not to overcook or pears will become mushy. Set aside.

❖ Remove pork from roasting pan. Cover with foil and allow to sit, 10 to 15 minutes. Spoon fat off the drippings in roasting pan. Discard any garlic that remains in pan. Place roasting pan on a burner over medium-high heat. When pork drippings are sizzling, deglaze pan by pouring in the red wine. Boil and reduce wine by half, stirring often and scraping bottom of pan with a spatula to incorporate all browned bits. Add red currant jelly, soy sauce, vinegar and cayenne. Season with salt to taste. Boil 2 to 3 minutes, until sauce thickens enough to coat the back of a spoon. Pour sauce over pears. Cook over medium heat just until pears are heated through.

❖ Slice pork roast into 1/2-inch slices. Spoon pears over pork and serve immediately.

MADISON PARK PORK MEDALLIONS
serves four

Ingredients

1	2-pound pork tenderloin
⅓	cup red wine
⅓	cup chicken stock
2	tablespoons Dijon mustard
1	tablespoon lemon juice, freshly squeezed
1	tablespoon mustard seed
2	medium cloves garlic, minced
1	teaspoon cumin
2	teaspoons Worcestershire sauce
¼	teaspoon salt
¼	teaspoon white pepper
⅛	teaspoon red pepper flakes
4	tablespoons cold butter
2	tablespoons fresh chives, chopped

Marinating time 2 hours. Preheat oven to broil.

❖ Cut pork into 8 equal slices. Place slices in a single layer in a shallow baking dish. In a small bowl, mix together remaining ingredients except butter and chives. Pour marinade over meat, cover and marinate in refrigerator 2 hours.

❖ Remove pork slices from marinade and place on a broiler pan. Pour marinade into a small saucepan and bring to a boil over high heat. Boil marinade until reduced by half. Turn heat down to low and swirl in butter a little at a time. Do not allow sauce to boil after butter has been added.

❖ Broil pork slices 3 minutes per side. Transfer pork to plates, allowing 2 slices per person. Spoon a little sauce over pork and sprinkle with chives. Serve immediately.

MUSTARD CRUMB PORK CHOPS
serves four

Ingredients

1 ½ cups fresh bread crumbs

1 cup fresh parsley, chopped

½ cup olive oil

2 tablespoons Dijon mustard

2 teaspoons dried thyme

salt and black pepper to taste

8 pork chops, 1 ½ inches thick

Preheat oven to broil.

❖ Mix first 5 ingredients together in a medium bowl. Season to taste with salt and pepper. Pat a portion of this crumb mixture onto both sides of each chop. (Can be prepared to this point several hours in advance. Keep refrigerated.) Place chops on a broiler pan, 4 inches from heat source. Broil, turning once with a spatula, until golden brown, about 3 minutes per side. Adjust oven to 350°. Bake chops 15–20 minutes. Serve immediately.

MUSTARD & CHUTNEY LAMB CHOPS
serves four

Ingredients

8 lamb chops

¼ cup Dijon mustard

¾ cup fruit chutney

1 cup dry white wine

½ teaspoon dried oregano

8 fresh sage leaves or ½ teaspoon dried

Marinating time up to 24 hours. Prepare grill or preheat oven to broil.

❖ Arrange chops in a single layer in a shallow dish. Combine 2 tablespoons mustard with ¼ cup chutney and spread generously on each chop. Whisk together remaining ingredients, except fresh sage leaves, and pour over lamb chops. Place a fresh sage leaf on top of each chop. Cover and marinate several hours or overnight in refrigerator. Bring to room temperature before cooking. Remove sage leaves and grill to desired doneness, about 3 minutes per side for medium-rare.

LAMB STEW WITH ORANGE ZEST
serves eight

Ingredients

4	pounds lamb leg or rump meat
¾	cup flour
1½	teaspoons salt
¼	teaspoon black pepper
4	tablespoons vegetable oil
3	cups onion, sliced
1	tablespoon sugar
3	cups dry red wine
1	pound mushrooms, quartered
1	8-ounce can tomato puree
1	teaspoon dried basil
½	teaspoon dried thyme
2	teaspoons orange zest, grated
2	medium cloves garlic, minced
4	medium carrots

Preheat oven to 325°.

❖ Cut meat into 1-inch pieces. Combine flour, salt and pepper in a large plastic bag. Add meat to bag in batches and toss, coating pieces evenly. Heat 1 tablespoon oil in a large, heavy skillet over medium-high heat. Add ⅓ of the meat and cook until browned on all sides, stirring frequently, about 5 minutes. Transfer meat to a large, heavy Dutch oven. Repeat with remaining meat in 2 batches, adding 1 tablespoon oil to skillet for each batch. Transfer meat to Dutch oven as it browns.

❖ Reduce heat to medium. Add remaining tablespoon oil to same skillet. Add onions and sugar. Sauté, stirring frequently, until glazed and slightly browned, about 6 minutes. Add wine and cook 2 minutes, stirring constantly to scrape up all browned bits from bottom of pan. Pour over meat in Dutch oven. Add mushrooms, tomato puree, basil, thyme, orange zest and garlic to Dutch oven. Stir to combine. Cover and bake until meat is tender, about 2½ hours, stirring occasionally. Meanwhile, cut carrots into large matchsticks. Add carrots to stew for last 30 minutes. Add a small amount of red wine during last 30 minutes of cooking if stew is too dry.

A festive way to serve stew is in individual "bowls," made by hollowing out French bread rolls.

ASIAN MARINATED RACK OF LAMB

serves eight

2   racks of lamb (16
     chops total)

Marinade

1   8-ounce jar Hoisin
     sauce

½   cup honey

¼   cup Asian sesame oil

¼   cup dry sherry

¼   cup sesame seeds

¼   cup canned black
     beans, rinsed

2   teaspoons orange zest

1   teaspoon curry powder

Marinating time up to 24 hours. Preheat oven to 450°.

❖   Blend all marinade ingredients in food processor. Pour over lamb and marinate several hours or overnight. Roast lamb about 30 minutes, or until a meat thermometer registers between 145° and 150° for medium-rare. To serve, carve rack into individual chops. Serve 2 chops per person.

Seattle Art Museum Art Studio
The Junior League provided $100,000 for the development of an Art Studio classroom at the Seattle Art Museum. Volunteers work in the classroom and promote the program.

LEG OF LAMB STUFFED WITH SPINACH & HAZELNUTS

serves six to eight

1	boneless leg of lamb (3 to 3 ½ pounds)
¼	teaspoon salt
	black pepper to taste

Stuffing

⅓	cup hazelnuts
4	cups (packed) fresh spinach, washed, stems removed
1	tablespoon butter or margarine
1	medium clove garlic, minced
¾	cup fine, dry bread crumbs
⅓	cup golden raisins
1	large egg
½	+ ¼ teaspoon ground cumin
½	+ ¼ teaspoon ground cinnamon
⅛	teaspoon cayenne
1	tablespoon olive oil

Preheat oven to 350°.

❖ Butterfly cut the leg of lamb, or ask the butcher to do it for you. Pound meat to an even thickness. Sprinkle with salt and pepper.

❖ For Stuffing: toast hazelnuts in a 350° oven for 8 minutes. Allow to cool. Place nuts in a towel and rub together to remove as much of the dark brown husk as possible. Chop nuts coarsely. Increase oven temperature to 375°.

❖ Chop spinach coarsely and cook, uncovered, in a large saucepan with ½-inch of water, for 3 to 4 minutes, turning frequently so it cooks evenly. Drain cooked spinach thoroughly, pressing with back of a large spoon to remove as much moisture as possible. Melt butter in same pan in which spinach was cooked. Add garlic and sauté over medium heat 1 to 2 minutes. Remove from heat; add hazelnuts, spinach, bread crumbs, raisins, egg, ½ teaspoon cumin, ½ teaspoon cinnamon and cayenne. Mix thoroughly.

❖ Pat stuffing evenly over meat. Roll up from long end and tie with kitchen twine at 1-inch intervals. Place seam side down in a heavy roasting pan. Rub with remaining cumin, cinnamon and 1 tablespoon olive oil. Roast lamb, uncovered, about 20 minutes per pound or until an instant-read thermometer registers 120° for medium-rare.

continued on page 191

Sauce

½	cup onion, chopped
½	cup dry red wine
1	tablespoon honey
1	medium clove garlic, smashed
1	cinnamon stick
2	cups chicken stock
½	teaspoon Worcestershire sauce
¼	teaspoon ground cumin
¼	teaspoon salt
1	pinch cayenne
1½	tablespoons flour
1	tablespoon butter, softened

❖ For Sauce: combine onion, red wine, honey, garlic and cinnamon stick in a medium saucepan. Bring to a boil and continue to boil until liquid is syrupy. Add chicken stock, Worcestershire, cumin, salt and cayenne. Bring to a rolling boil and cook 5 minutes.

❖ In a small bowl, combine flour and butter to make a smooth paste. Slowly add this to the simmering sauce, stirring with a whisk. Cook until slightly thickened, about 5 more minutes. Set aside until lamb is done.

❖ When lamb is done, remove from pan and set on a carving board, tented with foil. Let rest 10 minutes before carving. Drain fat from roasting pan and discard. Set roasting pan on a burner over medium-high heat. Strain sauce into roasting pan. Discard onion, garlic and cinnamon stick. Stir sauce to incorporate lamb drippings, being sure to scrape bottom of roasting pan well. Slice the roast and serve with sauce on the side.

Asparagus with Orange Vinaigrette
194

Asparagus with Tarragon Mustard Sauce
195

Sesame Asparagus
195

Asparagus with Pickled Ginger & Shallots
196

Broccoli Walnut Stir-Fry
196

Tangerine Beets
197

Carrots with a Spritz
197

Julienne of Carrots & Snow Peas
198

Herb Garden Green Beans
199

Wild Mushroom Sauté
200

Honey-Mustard Walla Walla Sweets
201

Sautéed Peas with Basil & Bacon
202

Lemon-Roasted New Potatoes
202

Potatoes Gruyère
203

Parmesan Potato Wedges
203

Pesto Mashed Potatoes
204

Spinach & Red Pepper Timbales
205

Zucchini Cakes
206

Zucchini & Olive Toss
206

Summer Vegetable Couscous
207

Everyday Orzo
208

Baked Polenta with Cheese
209

Ginger Rice
210

Saffron Rice with Pine Nuts
211

Wild Rice Pancakes
212

Winter Wild Rice with Dried Cherries
213

ASPARAGUS WITH ORANGE VINAIGRETTE
serves six

1 ½   pounds fresh asparagus

Vinaigrette

¼   cup orange juice,
     freshly squeezed

2   tablespoons rice wine
     vinegar

1   tablespoon orange
     juice concentrate

1   tablespoon honey

2   teaspoons Dijon
     mustard

¼   teaspoon ground
     allspice

¼   teaspoon salt

⅛   teaspoon white pepper

⅓   cup canola or
     vegetable oil

2   teaspoons orange zest
     (optional)

To cook asparagus:

❖   Fill a large bowl with ice water and set aside. Trim off tough ends (about 1 inch) of asparagus and cut stalks to a uniform length. If stems are fat and tough, remove outer layer with a vegetable peeler. In a large pan of simmering (not boiling) water, cook asparagus until tender but not limp (between 30 seconds and 3 minutes, depending on size of asparagus). Immediately immerse cooked asparagus in ice water to stop cooking and set color. When completely cooled, drain on paper towels. Serve cold, at room temperature or warm. To serve warm, reheat asparagus in a few tablespoons water in a shallow pan. Do not cover or asparagus will turn gray.

❖   Make the vinaigrette by combining remaining ingredients except canola oil and orange zest. Add canola oil in a slow, thin stream, whisking constantly until emulsified.

❖   Arrange asparagus on a serving dish. Drizzle with vinaigrette, sprinkle with orange zest and serve.

❖   This recipe makes more vinaigrette than you will need. Store extra in the refrigerator up to one week. Also good drizzled over fresh fruit or tossed with a green salad.

ASPARAGUS WITH TARRAGON MUSTARD SAUCE

serves six

1½   pounds fresh asparagus

Sauce

2   tablespoons white wine vinegar

2   tablespoons Dijon mustard

½   teaspoon Worcestershire sauce

1   teaspoon dried tarragon

1   pinch of sugar

⅓   cup olive oil

Follow directions on page 194 for cooking asparagus.

❖   Make sauce by combining remaining ingredients, except oil, in a small bowl. Add oil in a slow, thin stream, whisking constantly, until emulsified.

❖   Arrange asparagus on a serving dish, drizzle with sauce and serve.

SESAME ASPARAGUS

serves six

1½   pounds fresh asparagus

Sauce

2   tablespoons soy sauce

2   tablespoons Asian sesame oil

¼   teaspoon sugar

1   medium clove garlic, minced

1   tablespoon sesame seeds

Follow directions on page 194 for cooking asparagus.

❖   In a small bowl, combine the soy sauce, sesame oil, sugar, and garlic. Mix well.

❖   Arrange asparagus on a serving dish. Pour sauce over asparagus. Sprinkle with sesame seeds and serve.

ASPARAGUS WITH PICKLED GINGER & SHALLOTS

serves six

1 ½   pounds fresh asparagus

Sauce

3   tablespoons white wine vinegar

2   tablespoons shallots, minced

1   teaspoon Dijon mustard

2 ½   tablespoons pickled ginger

¼   cup canola or vegetable oil

1   tablespoon fresh chives, minced

Follow directions on page 194 for cooking asparagus.

❖   Make the sauce by pureeing the vinegar, shallots, mustard and 1 ½ tablespoons pickled ginger in a blender or food processor. With machine running, add oil in a slow, thin stream.

❖   Divide sauce evenly among 6 plates. Arrange asparagus on top of sauce. Cut remaining pickled ginger into slivers. Sprinkle slivered ginger and chives over asparagus. Serve immediately.

BROCCOLI WALNUT STIR-FRY

serves six

Ingredients

3   tablespoons Asian sesame oil

½   cup walnuts, coarsely chopped

6   cups broccoli florets

1   cup red bell pepper, diced

2   tablespoons soy sauce

❖   Heat oil in a large skillet over medium heat. Add walnuts and sauté 1 minute. Add broccoli and red pepper. Cook, stirring often, until broccoli is tender, about 6 minutes. Add soy sauce for last minute of cooking. Serve immediately.

TANGERINE BEETS
serves four

6 medium beets

Sauce

1 tablespoon olive oil

4 tablespoons tangerine
or orange juice, freshly
squeezed

2 tablespoons green
onion, chopped

2 tablespoons fresh
chives, minced

1½ teaspoons red wine
vinegar

salt and pepper

⅓ cup olive oil

Preheat oven to 350°.

❖ Cut off greens and pointed root ends of beets. If beets are large, cut in half or thirds. Rub beets with 1 tablespoon oil and place in a shallow baking dish. Add about ¼ inch of water to dish. Cover tightly with foil and bake until tender throughout when tested with a skewer or knife, 45 to 60 minutes. When cool enough to handle, peel beets with a small knife and cut into ½-inch dice.

❖ In a small bowl, thoroughly combine tangerine juice, green onion, chives, vinegar, salt and pepper. Add oil in a slow stream, whisking constantly until emulsified. Toss beets with sauce and serve. Can be served warm, at room temperature or chilled.

CARROTS WITH A SPRITZ
serves six

Ingredients

1 pound carrots

2 tablespoons butter

2 tablespoons lemon
juice, freshly squeezed

1 tablespoon lemon zest

1 tablespoon sugar

salt and pepper

2 tablespoons fresh
parsley, finely chopped

❖ Peel carrots and quarter lengthwise. Cut quarters into 2-inch strips. Cook carrots in boiling water until almost tender, about 3 minutes. Drain and return to pan. Add butter, lemon juice, lemon zest, sugar, salt and pepper. Stir to combine. Cook over medium-high heat for 3 to 4 minutes until carrots are glazed. Toss with parsley and serve.

JULIENNE OF CARROTS & SNOW PEAS
serves six

Ingredients

3	cups carrots, julienned
1 ½	cups snow peas, julienned
1	tablespoon Asian sesame oil
2	tablespoons green onion, chopped
1	medium clove garlic, minced
1	teaspoon fresh ginger, minced (optional)
	salt and white pepper to taste

❖ Fill a medium bowl with ice water and set aside. Cook carrots in boiling water for 2 minutes. Add snow peas and cook 2 minutes more. Drain vegetables and immerse immediately in ice water to stop cooking and set colors. When vegetables are completely cool, drain thoroughly.

❖ Heat oil in medium skillet over medium-high heat. Add carrots, snow peas, green onion, garlic, and ginger. Stir fry 1 to 2 minutes. Season with salt and white pepper. Serve immediately.

❖ Do-ahead Hint: parboil the julienned vegetables ahead of time; keep refrigerated. Stir fry at the last minute.

❖ For a milder flavor, substitute olive oil and/or butter for the sesame oil and omit the ginger.

To julienne vegetables, cut them into even sections 2-3 inches long. Cut each section into thin slices lengthwise, then cut slices into thin strips.

HERB GARDEN GREEN BEANS
serves six

Ingredients

1	pound fresh green beans
4	tablespoons butter or margarine
⅓	cup onion, finely chopped
¼	cup celery, minced
¼	cup fresh parsley, minced
¼	cup fresh basil, slivered or 2 teaspoons dried
1	teaspoon fresh rosemary or ¼ teaspoon dried
1	medium clove garlic, minced
½	teaspoon salt

❖ Fill a large bowl with ice water and set aside. Trim and clean beans. Cook in a large pot of boiling water until tender but not limp, about 4 to 5 minutes. Immediately immerse cooked beans in ice water to stop cooking and set color. When completely cool, drain beans thoroughly.

❖ Melt butter in a large pan over medium heat. Add onion and celery. Cook until soft but not browned, about 5 minutes. Add remaining ingredients, except beans, and cook 3 minutes longer. Add beans, toss to combine. Cook, uncovered, until beans are heated through. Serve immediately.

To sliver basil leaves, roll several leaves of similar size into a tight cylinder and slice crosswise into thin strips.

WILD MUSHROOM SAUTÉ
serves four

Ingredients

4	slices thick bacon, slivered
1	cup onion, chopped
1	pound fresh chanterelle mushrooms, coarsely chopped
	salt and pepper to taste
¼	cup fresh parsley, chopped

❖ In a large sauté pan over medium heat, sauté bacon until translucent. Drain off all but 2 tablespoons bacon drippings. Add onion to pan and sauté until soft but not brown, about 5 minutes. Add chanterelles and sauté until soft and browned, about 15 minutes. Season with salt and pepper, sprinkle with parsley. Serve immediately.

This recipe works well with any wild mushroom. In Washington, fall is the season for porcini, oyster and shiitake. Spring brings the delectable morel.

HONEY-MUSTARD WALLA WALLA SWEETS
serves six

Ingredients

¼	cup currants
3	tablespoons red wine vinegar
4	large onions, preferably Walla Walla Sweets
4	tablespoons butter or margarine
2	tablespoons Dijon mustard
2	tablespoons honey
1	teaspoon paprika
½	teaspoon salt
¼	teaspoon ground cloves

Preheat oven to 350°.

❖ Soak currants in vinegar 10 minutes. Cut each onion lengthwise into eighths. Place onions in a shallow roasting pan. Melt butter or margarine in a small saucepan; stir in currants, vinegar and remaining ingredients. Pour over onions, stirring and breaking up onions so they are coated on all sides. Bake until onions are soft and glazed, about 30 minutes. Serve warm.

Walla Walla onions, grown in Walla Walla, Washington, are golden in color and sweet in flavor. They are available through June and July. Comparable varieties are the Maui Onion from Hawaii, and the Vidalia from Georgia.

SAUTÉED PEAS WITH BASIL & BACON
serves six

Ingredients

2	slices thick bacon, cut into slivers
½	tablespoon olive oil
2	medium cloves garlic, minced
2	tablespoons shallots, minced
1	16-ounce package frozen peas, thawed
½	cup fresh basil leaves, slivered
	salt and pepper to taste

❖ Sauté bacon in a large skillet over medium heat. When bacon is crisp, remove with a slotted spoon and drain on paper towels. Using the same pan, pour off all but 1 tablespoon bacon drippings, add olive oil and sauté garlic and shallots for 2 minutes. Add peas and basil. Cook until peas are heated through, 4 to 5 minutes. Just before serving, add cooked bacon and season with salt and pepper to taste.

LEMON-ROASTED NEW POTATOES
serves four

Ingredients

1	pound medium, red new potatoes
¼	cup olive oil
2	tablespoons lemon juice, freshly squeezed
1	tablespoon fresh oregano, minced
2	teaspoons lemon zest
½	teaspoon salt
¼	teaspoon pepper
6	small bay leaves

Preheat oven to 375°.

❖ Quarter potatoes and place in a baking dish in a single layer. In a small bowl, blend remaining ingredients, except bay leaves. Pour over potatoes. Distribute whole bay leaves evenly among potatoes. Roast 45 minutes or until tender, turning occasionally with a spatula. Discard bay leaves. Serve hot.

POTATOES GRUYÈRE
serves six

Ingredients

4	medium baking potatoes (about 2 pounds)
1 ½	cups Gruyère cheese, shredded
¼	cup half and half
3	tablespoons fresh chives, coarsely chopped
2	tablespoons butter or margarine, melted
	pinch of nutmeg
	salt and black pepper to taste

Preheat oven to 350°.

❖ Butter an 8x10-inch baking dish. Bring a large pot of water to a rolling boil over high heat. Scrub potatoes but do not peel. Cut into quarters. Add potatoes to water, reduce heat to medium and cook 10 to 15 minutes or until potatoes are very tender. Drain and coarsely mash potatoes with a fork. Mix in remaining ingredients, except ¼ cup of cheese. Spread potatoes evenly in prepared dish. Sprinkle remaining cheese on top. Bake 25 minutes. Brown under broiler if necessary. Serve immediately.

PARMESAN POTATO WEDGES
serves six

Ingredients

4	large baking potatoes
¼	cup olive oil
¼	cup Parmesan cheese, grated
1	teaspoon salt
1	teaspoon paprika
½	teaspoon freshly ground pepper

Preheat oven to 375°.

❖ Scrub unpeeled potatoes and cut into wedges. Place wedges, skin side down, in a single layer in a large baking dish. Mix remaining ingredients together in a small bowl. Brush evenly over potatoes and bake for 1 hour, or until potatoes are tender when pierced with a fork. Serve hot.

PESTO MASHED POTATOES
serves six

Ingredients

2½	pounds baking potatoes
6	tablespoons butter or margarine
½	cup sour cream
⅓	cup Pesto Sauce
	salt and white pepper to taste

Pesto Sauce

2	medium cloves garlic
2	cups fresh basil leaves, cleaned and dried
½	cup olive oil
¼	cup pine nuts
½	teaspoon salt
½	cup Parmesan or Asiago cheese, grated

❖ Bring a large pot of water to a boil. Peel potatoes and cut into large dice. Add potatoes to boiling water, cook until tender, 15 to 20 minutes, and drain. Transfer potatoes to a large bowl and mash with a potato masher, or press through a potato ricer into a large bowl. Stir in butter, sour cream and ⅓ cup pesto. Season with salt and white pepper. Potatoes can be kept warm by placing bowl over a large pot of simmering water. Cover bowl with aluminum foil. Serve potatoes warm.

❖ For Pesto Sauce: with machine running, drop garlic through feed tube of a food processor and mince finely. Add remaining ingredients, except cheese. Puree to a smooth paste, scraping down a few times with a spatula. Transfer to a small bowl and stir in cheese. This recipe makes more pesto than needed for this dish. Freeze leftover pesto for up to six months.

Freeze pesto in ice cube trays then store in freezer bags, using only as many "cubes" as needed at a time.

SPINACH & RED PEPPER TIMBALES

serves eight

Ingredients

1	tablespoon butter or margarine
1	cup red bell pepper, diced
4	cups tightly packed, fresh, cleaned spinach or
1	10-ounce package frozen spinach
1	10-ounce package frozen peas
¼	cup fresh parsley, chopped
¾	cup chicken stock
1	teaspoon sugar
½	teaspoon salt
	black pepper to taste
3	large eggs, slightly beaten

Preheat oven to 350°.

❖　Butter 8 small timbale molds or ramekins. Set aside. Melt butter in a small sauté pan over medium-low heat. Sauté red pepper until tender. Set aside. In a food processor, puree spinach, peas, parsley, chicken stock, sugar, salt and pepper.

❖　Combine puree with bell pepper and eggs. Divide mixture evenly among prepared molds. Place molds in a baking pan and add enough hot water to reach half way up sides of molds. Bake 35 minutes or until a tester inserted in the center comes out clean. To serve, run a knife around the sides of each mold and invert directly onto plates.

❖　Timbales may be made 1 day in advance and refrigerated in their molds. To reheat, preheat oven to 450°. Place molds in a water bath, as before, and heat in oven for 15 to 20 minutes. Unmold just before serving.

Timbale molds are round, high-sided and usually made of aluminum. Individual-sized molds have a ½ cup capacity.

ZUCCHINI CAKES
serves four

2   cups zucchini, shredded

2   large eggs

¼   cup onion, minced

½   cup flour

¼   cup Parmesan cheese, grated

½   teaspoon salt

½   teaspoon oregano

¼   teaspoon white pepper

        olive oil

        sour cream, tomato, diced (optional)

Preheat oven to warm.

❖   In a medium bowl, combine zucchini, eggs and onion. In a separate bowl, combine flour, Parmesan, salt, oregano and white pepper. Blend dry ingredients into zucchini mixture, mixing well. Lightly oil a large, heavy skillet and place over medium-high heat. When skillet is hot, drop in mixture by the heaping tablespoonful. Cook until browned on both sides and cooked through, about 2 minutes per side. Keep pancakes covered with foil in warm oven while cooking remaining batter. Serve warm with a small dollop of sour cream and sprinkling of diced tomato.

ZUCCHINI & OLIVE TOSS
serves four

1   large red bell pepper

2   tablespoons butter or margarine

1   pound zucchini

16   olives, preferably Kalamata

        salt and black pepper

❖   Cut red pepper into ½-inch pieces and cook in butter, covered, over medium-low heat for about 5 minutes. Cut zucchini in half lengthwise, then into ¼-inch slices. Pit olives, if necessary, and cut into quarters. Add zucchini and olives to peppers. Cook, covered, stirring occasionally, about 5 minutes, or until zucchini is just tender. Season with salt and pepper. Serve immediately.

SUMMER VEGETABLE COUSCOUS

serves six

Ingredients

1	small red bell pepper
2	tablespoons butter or margarine
1	teaspoon olive oil
1 ¼	cups carrot, shredded
½	cup onion, chopped
1 ¼	cups zucchini, shredded
¼	cup fresh parsley, chopped
2	tablespoons lemon juice, freshly squeezed
½	teaspoon dried savory
¼	teaspoon dried rosemary
½	cup chicken stock or water
½	teaspoon salt
¾	cup couscous, uncooked

❖ Cut red pepper into ¼-inch strips. Melt butter and oil in a large skillet over medium heat. Add red pepper, carrots and onion. Sauté 5 minutes. Add zucchini and sauté 5 minutes more. Stir in parsley, lemon juice, savory and rosemary.

❖ Meanwhile, combine chicken stock or water with salt in a small saucepan, cover and bring to a boil. Stir in couscous, remove from heat, cover and let stand 5 minutes or until all liquid is absorbed. Fluff couscous with a fork to separate grains. Add couscous to vegetable mixture, stir well and serve.

Although couscous looks like a grain, it is actually a pasta made from coarsely-ground semolina flour. Use it in place of rice or potatoes.

EVERYDAY ORZO
serves four to six

Ingredients

4	tablespoons butter or margarine
1	cup onion, chopped
2	medium cloves garlic, minced
2½	cups chicken stock
2	cups orzo pasta, uncooked
½	cup Gruyère cheese, shredded
2	tablespoons fresh chives, chopped
	salt and pepper to taste

❖ Melt butter in a large, heavy skillet over medium-low heat. Add onion and cook until soft but not browned, about 6 minutes. Add garlic and cook 2 minutes more. Meanwhile, in a medium saucepan, heat chicken stock to boiling.

❖ Add orzo to onion and garlic in skillet. Stir in hot chicken stock, bring to a boil, cover and remove from heat. Let stand, without removing cover, until all liquid is absorbed, about 25 minutes. Stir in cheese until melted; add chives and season with salt and pepper. Orzo will have a creamy consistency. Serve hot.

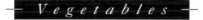

BAKED POLENTA WITH CHEESE

serves six

Ingredients

2	cups chicken stock
1 ½	cups water
1	teaspoon salt
1	cup yellow cornmeal
2	tablespoons butter or margarine
1	cup Monterey Jack or Swiss cheese, shredded
¼	cup Parmesan cheese, grated

Preheat oven to 350°.

❖ Bring chicken stock, water and salt to a boil in a medium saucepan. Reduce heat to a simmer and add cornmeal in a slow stream, stirring constantly. Cook, stirring often, 7 to 10 minutes over medium-low heat. Polenta will become thick.

❖ Pour polenta into a shallow baking pan and smooth to an even layer. Cool 15 to 20 minutes in refrigerator. Cut cooled polenta into 2-inch squares and arrange squares like fallen dominos in a shallow, broiler-proof baking dish. Dot with butter and sprinkle cheeses evenly over the top. Bake 15 to 20 minutes or until polenta is heated through. If polenta is not browned on top, it can be run quickly under the broiler until golden. Serve immediately.

Dress this polenta up with a topping of Wild Mushroom Sauté (page 200) or Terrific Tomato Sauce (page 107).

GINGER RICE
serves four

2   cups chicken stock

1   tablespoon butter or margarine

½   teaspoon salt

1   cup rice

2   teaspoons vegetable oil

¼   cup carrots, diced

¼   cup green onion, chopped

2   medium cloves garlic, minced

1   tablespoon fresh ginger, minced

2   tablespoons soy sauce

1   teaspoon ground coriander

❖   In a medium saucepan, boil chicken stock, butter and salt. Stir in rice, cover, reduce heat, and simmer 20 to 25 minutes. Meanwhile, heat oil in a small skillet over medium heat and sauté carrots 2 minutes. Add green onion, garlic and ginger. Sauté 3 minutes more. Set aside. When rice is cooked, stir in carrot/onion mixture, soy sauce and coriander. Serve hot.

Ginger root does not require peeling before use. Clean, cut into quarter-sized knobs and drop into bowl of food processor with motor running to mince.

SAFFRON RICE WITH PINE NUTS

serves four

Ingredients

⅓	cup pine nuts
2	tablespoons butter or margarine
½	cup onion, finely chopped
2	medium cloves garlic, minced
1	teaspoon saffron threads or ¼ teaspoon powdered saffron
1	cup rice, uncooked
2	cups chicken stock
2	tablespoons fresh parsley, finely chopped

❖ Toast pine nuts by sautéing them in a small, dry skillet over medium heat about 2 minutes or until they are golden. Set aside.

❖ Melt butter in a medium saucepan over medium heat. Add onion and cook until soft but not brown, about 5 minutes. Add garlic and saffron, cook 2 minutes longer. Add rice and stir to coat. Add chicken stock, bring to a boil, cover, reduce heat and simmer 17 to 20 minutes, until rice is tender. Stir in parsley and pine nuts. Serve immediately.

It is best to buy saffron threads rather than powder. Powdered saffron is apt to be mixed with fillers and loses its flavor more quickly. Always crush saffron threads before using.

WILD RICE PANCAKES
serves four

1 ½   cups wild rice, cooked

⅓   cup milk

2   tablespoons flour

2   tablespoons fresh parsley, minced

1   tablespoon shallot, finely minced

1   medium clove garlic, minced

1   large egg

½   teaspoon baking powder

½   teaspoon dried basil

¼   teaspoon salt

4   tablespoons butter or margarine, melted

1   tablespoon vegetable oil

sour cream (optional)

fresh chives or parsley (optional)

Preheat oven to warm.

❖   Place all ingredients, except 2 tablespoons butter and the oil, in the bowl of a food processor. Pulse machine a few times to blend mixture into a coarse batter. Be careful not to overprocess. Heat some of the remaining melted butter and oil in a medium skillet over medium heat. Drop batter by large spoonfuls into hot pan and cook until browned and set. Turn and cook the other side until browned and pancake is cooked through, about 2 minutes per side. Keep pancakes covered with foil in a warm oven while cooking remaining batter. Add remaining butter and oil to pan as necessary. Serve pancakes with a small dollop of sour cream and a sprinkling of chives or parsley.

Adding a little oil to butter when sauteing will prevent the butter from burning as easily and allow cooking at a higher temperature.

WINTER WILD RICE WITH DRIED CHERRIES

serves six

Ingredients

2	tablespoons butter or margarine
½	cup shallot, chopped
2⅔	cups chicken stock
½	pound wild rice
1	teaspoon dried thyme
½	cup hazelnuts
¾	cup dried cherries
2	tablespoons fresh parsley, chopped

Preheat oven to 350°.

❖ Melt butter in a medium saucepan over medium heat. Sauté shallot until soft but not brown, about 5 minutes. Add chicken stock, increase heat to high and bring to a boil. Add rice and thyme, reduce heat to low, cover and cook 40 minutes.

❖ Meanwhile, toast hazelnuts on a baking sheet for 8 minutes. While still warm, place nuts in a towel and rub together to remove as much of the dark brown husk as possible. Chop nuts coarsely.

❖ Add nuts and cherries to rice, cover and continue cooking 15 minutes or until rice is tender and all stock has been absorbed. Rice should be glossy and moist. Sprinkle with parsley and serve immediately.

For a delicious variation of this recipe, substitute dried cranberries for the cherries.

Desserts

Espresso Chip Cookies
216

Hazelnut Cinnamon Crisps
217

Better-Than-Mom's Oatmeal Cookies
218

Special Mention Biscotti
219

Lemon Pistachio Snaps
220

Almond Thins
221

Cranberry Walnut Bars
222

Zebra Bars
224

Oat-Bottomed Brownies
225

Triple Chocolate Raspberry Brownies
226

Dark & White Brownies
227

Coffee & Cream Cake
228

Fresh Ginger Cake
229

Hazelnut Mocha Mousse Roll
230

Berry Patch Shortcakes
232

Purple Plum Cheese Tart
233

Lemon-Ginger Cheesecake
234

White Chocolate Raspberry Cheesecake
236

Praline Brie
237

Apple Pie Americana
238

Almond à la Tarte
239

Cranberry Crumb Tart
240

Raspberry Tart
242

Strawberry Almond Torte
243

Apple Bread Pudding with Cider Sauce
244

Apple Blackberry Crisp
245

Rhubarberry Crisp
246

Plum Crisp
246

Whidbey Island Soufflés
247

Frozen Espresso Cream
248

Chocolate Orange Sorbet
248

Fruit Sorbet with Blackberry Coulis
249

ESPRESSO CHIP COOKIES
makes twenty-four cookies

Ingredients

1 ¼ cups flour

½ teaspoon baking powder

½ teaspoon cinnamon

⅛ teaspoon salt

½ cup butter or margarine

⅓ cup brown sugar, packed

⅓ cup sugar

1 large egg

5 teaspoons instant espresso powder, divided

2 teaspoons vanilla

1 cup semi-sweet chocolate chips

½ cup walnuts, chopped

Chilling time 1 hour. Preheat oven to 350°.

❖ In a medium bowl, stir together flour, baking powder, cinnamon and salt. In a large bowl, using a wooden spoon, cream together butter and sugars until combined. Stir in egg. In a small bowl, dissolve 3 teaspoons espresso powder in vanilla. Stir espresso mixture into butter mixture until blended; fold in flour mixture and combine thoroughly. Stir in chocolate chips and nuts. Cover and refrigerate dough 1 hour.

❖ Lightly butter 2 baking sheets. Drop dough by large spoonfuls onto prepared baking sheets, leaving 2 inches between cookies. Sprinkle with remaining espresso powder. Bake one sheet at a time, 9 to 12 minutes, or until cookies are lightly browned on bottom. Cool on baking sheets 5 minutes before transferring cookies to racks.

HAZELNUT CINNAMON CRISPS
makes eighty cookies

Ingredients

1 1/4	cups hazelnuts
3/4	cup butter or margarine, chilled
1 1/4	cups powdered sugar
1	teaspoon cinnamon
1	large egg
2	cups flour

Preheat oven to 350°. Chilling time 30 minutes to 2 days.

❖ Place hazelnuts on a baking sheet and toast until fragrant, about 10 minutes. Cool. Chop in food processor until fine but not ground.

❖ Cut butter into cubes. Place hazelnuts, butter, sugar and cinnamon in a medium bowl. Using an electric mixer, beat until combined. Blend in egg. With mixer set on lowest speed, add flour, beating until combined. Gather dough into a smooth ball, adding a little more flour, if necessary, and transfer to a flat work surface, lined with a sheet of parchment paper. Form dough into a 4 x 8-inch loaf, about 1 1/4-inches tall. Wrap loaf in parchment paper as you would wrap a package, keeping corners square. Refrigerate at least 30 minutes or up to 2 days.

❖ Unwrap dough and line 2 baking sheets with parchment paper. Using a sharp knife, cut chilled dough into 4 equal pieces. Cut each piece into approximately 20 rectangular cookies, each about 1/4-inch thick. Place cookies on prepared baking sheets, spacing 1/2-inch apart.

❖ Bake until edges just start to turn brown, about 12 minutes. Cool on wire racks.

BETTER-THAN-MOM'S OATMEAL COOKIES
makes about forty-eight cookies

Ingredients

1	cup butter or margarine
1	cup sugar
1	cup dark brown sugar
2	large eggs
2	teaspoons vanilla
1 ½	cups flour
1 ⅛	teaspoons baking soda
1	teaspoon salt
1	teaspoon ground cinnamon
½	teaspoon ground mace
½	teaspoon nutmeg
½	teaspoon ground cloves
3	cups oatmeal, uncooked
1	cup walnuts or pecans, chopped
1	cup yellow raisins, finely chopped

Preheat oven to 350°.

❖ Cream butter, sugar and brown sugar, with electric mixer until light and fluffy. Add eggs and vanilla, mix thoroughly. In a separate bowl, sift together flour, soda, salt and spices. With mixer running, gradually add dry ingredients to butter/sugar mixture. Continue mixing until thoroughly combined. Fold in oatmeal, nuts and raisins by hand. Drop by tablespoons, 2 inches apart, onto a lightly greased cookie sheet, flattening each mound slightly. Bake 8 to 10 minutes for a soft cookie, 12 minutes for a crunchy cookie. Cool on racks.

Happy Birthdays / Seattle Emergency Housing
Junior League volunteers host birthday parties and donate needed items for children at the Seattle Emergency Housing Service shelter.

SPECIAL MENTION BISCOTTI
makes twenty-eight cookies

7	tablespoons unsalted butter
½	cup plus 2 tablespoons sugar
1	large egg
1	egg yolk
½	teaspoon vanilla extract
1	cup flour
1	teaspoon baking powder
¼	teaspoon salt
1½	cups almonds, toasted and coarsely chopped
1	teaspoon orange zest, grated

Preheat oven to 375°.

❖ In a large mixing bowl, cream butter and sugar until light and fluffy. Beat in egg, egg yolk and vanilla.

❖ In a small bowl, combine flour, baking powder and salt. Sift into butter mixture. Gently fold in almonds and orange zest.

❖ Transfer to a floured surface and shape into 2 slightly flattened logs, each 3x14-inches. (If dough is too soft, refrigerate 1 hour before shaping.)

❖ Place logs side by side on buttered baking sheet. Bake in preheated oven 10 to 12 minutes. Remove from oven, reduce oven temperature to 325°.

❖ Cut each log diagonally into ½-inch wide strips. Place each strip on its side on the baking sheet. Return to oven, bake 10 to 15 minutes until golden.

If you prefer, substitute hazelnuts for the almonds... or even chocolate chips.

LEMON PISTACHIO SNAPS
makes sixty cookies

2   cups flour

½   teaspoon baking soda

¼   teaspoon salt

¾   cup butter or margarine, softened

¾   cup plus 3 tablespoons sugar, divided

1   large egg

1   tablespoon lemon zest, grated

1   tablespoon lemon juice

⅓   cup pistachio nuts, finely chopped

Chilling time 1 hour. Preheat oven to 350°.

❖ In a large bowl, sift together flour, baking soda and salt. Set aside.

❖ Cream butter and ¾ cup sugar until light and fluffy. Beat in egg, mixing until just combined. Add lemon zest and juice. Blend in dry ingredients, mix to thoroughly combine. Wrap dough in plastic and chill for 1 hour.

❖ Combine pistachio nuts and remaining sugar in small bowl. Shape dough into 1-inch balls. Roll balls in pistachio-sugar mixture. Place 2 inches apart on ungreased baking sheets. Press cookies down with a small glass to flatten slightly. Bake 10 to 12 minutes until golden. Transfer to racks to cool.

A zester, used for removing the outer skin of citrus fruits, peels away strips of zest, leaving the bitter white pith behind. Dice strips when grated zest is needed.

ALMOND THINS
makes forty squares

Ingredients

1   cup unsalted butter, softened

1   cup sugar

1   large egg, separated

1½ tablespoons almond liqueur

2   teaspoons orange zest, grated

¼   teaspoon salt

2   cups flour

¾   cup sliced almonds

Preheat oven to 300°.

❖   In a large bowl, beat butter and sugar together until light and creamy, about 5 minutes. Add egg yolk, almond liqueur, orange zest and salt; beat until combined. Stir in flour and blend well. Pat dough evenly into a 10x15-inch jelly roll pan.

❖   In a small bowl, beat egg white until foamy. Brush over dough. Sprinkle almonds evenly over top and pat gently into dough.

❖   Bake in preheated oven 40 minutes, or until lightly golden. While still warm, cut into 2-inch squares and transfer to a wire rack to cool.

These delicate cookies will keep for up to two weeks at room temperature when stored in a tightly covered tin.

CRANBERRY WALNUT BARS
makes thirty-six bars

Crust

2	cups flour
½	cup plus 1 teaspoon sugar, divided
12	tablespoons unsalted butter, chilled
1	large egg, beaten
2	tablespoons milk

Filling

¾	cup walnuts
1	12-ounce bag fresh cranberries
1	cup water
1¼	cups sugar
2	tablespoons unsalted butter
1	tablespoon almond liqueur (optional)

Chilling time 1 hour. Preheat oven to 300°.

❖   For Crust: combine flour and ½ cup sugar in a mixer, blender or food processor. Add butter in small pieces and blend quickly, just until mixture resembles coarse meal. Blend egg and milk together; pour into flour mixture and mix just until dough comes together. Divide dough into 2 equal portions. Wrap in plastic and refrigerate 1 hour.

❖   For Filling: spread walnuts on a baking sheet and toast in oven for 5 minutes. Remove from oven and increase temperature to 375°.

❖   In a medium saucepan, bring cranberries, water and sugar to a boil. Reduce heat and simmer until berries have broken down and syrup has thickened, about 15 minutes. Remove from heat and stir in butter. Add almond liqueur, if desired. Cover pan and set aside to allow berries to cool and thicken.

continued on page 223

❖   Coarsely chop walnuts and stir into cranberries.

❖   Lightly grease a 9x13-inch baking pan. Remove dough from refrigerator and work with hands until pliable. On a floured surface, roll one half into a 10x14-inch rectangle. Lift it by wrapping around the rolling pin, then unroll over prepared pan. Press dough evenly over bottom and ½ inch up sides. Repair any cracks by pressing together with fingers.

❖   Pour cooled cranberry mixture over bottom crust. Roll remaining dough as above and place over filling. Trim away excess dough. Press down on top layer gently to fuse the layers. Sprinkle with remaining sugar.

❖   Bake on middle rack in oven until edges are golden brown and center is light brown, 25 to 30 minutes. Cool and cut into squares.

ZEBRA BARS
makes twenty-four bars

Ingredients

¾	cup butter
6	ounces unsweetened chocolate
4	large eggs
4	teaspoons orange-flavored liqueur
1	teaspoon vanilla extract
2	cups sugar
1	cup flour

Frosting

½	cup butter, softened
1 ½	cups powdered sugar
2	tablespoons orange-flavored liqueur
½	teaspoon vanilla extract

Glaze

1	ounce unsweetened chocolate
1	teaspoon butter

Preheat oven to 350°. Chilling time 1 hour.

❖ In a small, heavy saucepan, heat butter and chocolate until melted, stirring constantly. Remove from heat and allow to cool.

❖ In a large bowl, beat eggs, liqueur and vanilla extract until thick and lemon-colored. Gradually add sugar, beating until mixture is very light and fluffy. Add chocolate mixture and blend well. Fold in flour and mix gently until thoroughly combined. Spread into a greased 9x13-inch pan. Bake in preheated oven for 25 minutes. Remove from oven and cool completely before frosting.

❖ For Frosting: beat butter in a small bowl until fluffy. Add powdered sugar, orange liqueur and vanilla extract. Beat until smooth and creamy. Spread evenly over cooled brownies.

❖ For Glaze: combine chocolate and butter in a small, heavy saucepan. Melt over low heat, stirring constantly. Drizzle glaze in a diagonal pattern over frosted brownies. Cover with plastic wrap and refrigerate until firm before cutting, about 1 hour.

OAT-BOTTOMED BROWNIES
makes thirty brownies

Oat Base

2	cups rolled oats
¾	cup flour
½	cup brown sugar
¼	teaspoon baking powder
¼	teaspoon salt
⅔	cup butter or margarine, melted

Brownies

2	cups walnuts, chopped
14	ounces bittersweet chocolate
4	ounces semi-sweet chocolate
2	ounces unsweetened chocolate
1	cup butter or margarine
¼	cup cocoa powder
1	cup sugar
¾	cup brown sugar, firmly packed
4	large eggs
1	tablespoon vanilla
1	cup flour
¼	teaspoon salt

Preheat oven to 350°.

❖ For Base: butter a 9x13-inch baking dish. In a large bowl, combine oats, flour, brown sugar, baking powder and salt. Add butter and stir until thoroughly combined. Press mixture evenly into bottom of prepared pan. Bake 12 minutes. Cool.

❖ For Brownies: place walnuts on a baking sheet. Toast in oven 10 minutes. Set aside. Chop chocolates coarsely. In top of a double boiler, over hot, not simmering water, melt chocolates with butter and cocoa powder, stirring occasionally, until smooth. Remove top portion of double boiler and cool mixture to lukewarm, about 10 minutes.

❖ In a large bowl, beat sugars and eggs with an electric mixer at high speed until mixture is thick and light colored, about 5 minutes. Beat in vanilla. Add chocolate mixture and mix until well combined. With mixer on low speed, beat in flour and salt until just combined. Stir in walnuts.

❖ Pour batter over baked oat base, spread evenly with a spatula. Bake until a tester inserted 2 inches from center comes out slightly moist, about 40 to 45 minutes. Cool brownies completely in pan on a rack before cutting into squares.

TRIPLE CHOCOLATE RASPBERRY BROWNIES
makes twenty brownies

10	ounces bittersweet chocolate
3	ounces semi-sweet chocolate
2	ounces unsweetened chocolate
1	cup butter or margarine
¼	cup cocoa powder
1	cup sugar
¾	cup brown sugar, packed
3	large eggs
½	cup raspberry liqueur
2	teaspoons vanilla
1¼	cups flour
¼	teaspoon salt
2	tablespoons powdered sugar

Preheat oven to 350°.

❖ Butter a 9x13-inch baking pan. Chop chocolates coarsely. In top of a double boiler, over hot, not simmering, water, melt chocolates with butter and cocoa powder, stirring occasionally, until smooth. Remove top portion of double boiler and cool mixture to lukewarm, about 10 minutes.

❖ In a large bowl, beat sugars and eggs with an electric mixer at high speed until thick and light colored, about 5 minutes. Beat in liqueur and vanilla. Add chocolate mixture and mix until well-blended. With mixer on low speed, beat in flour and salt just until combined.

❖ Pour batter into prepared pan and smooth surface with rubber spatula. Bake 25 to 30 minutes or until toothpick inserted 2 inches from center comes out slightly moist. Cool brownies in pan on a wire rack. When completely cool, cut brownies into squares. Place powdered sugar in a sieve and dust brownies after cutting.

DARK & WHITE BROWNIES
makes sixteen brownies

Ingredients

½	cup butter or margarine
8	ounces white chocolate chips
2	large eggs
½	cup sugar
1	cup flour
½	teaspoon vanilla
½	teaspoon salt
½	cup semi-sweet chocolate chips

Preheat oven to 350°.

❖ Butter bottom and sides of an 8-inch square pan. Line bottom of pan with parchment paper or foil. Butter paper. Melt butter in a small saucepan over low heat. Add half the white chocolate chips; do not stir.

❖ In a medium bowl, beat eggs with an electric mixer until frothy. Gradually add sugar and continue beating until mixture is pale and thickened, about 6 minutes. Add white chocolate mixture, flour, vanilla and salt. Mix until just combined. Stir in remaining white chocolate chips and semi-sweet chips. Spoon mixture into prepared pan. Smooth top with spatula. Bake until tester inserted in center comes out almost clean, about 30 minutes. Cover with foil if brownies brown too quickly. Cool brownies in pan on a wire rack. Cut into squares when completely cool.

COFFEE & CREAM CAKE

serves ten

Cake

2	cups flour
1	teaspoon baking powder
½	teaspoon baking soda
¼	teaspoon salt
¾	cup butter or margarine, softened
1	cup sugar
2	large eggs
2	teaspoons vanilla
1	cup sour cream
2	tablespoons instant espresso powder
1	tablespoon hot water

Glaze

3	tablespoons brewed coffee
2	teaspoons instant espresso powder
¾	cup powdered sugar

Preheat oven to 350°.

❖ Generously butter a 1½-quart bundt pan. Set aside.

❖ For Cake: in a medium bowl, sift together flour, baking powder, baking soda and salt. In a separate bowl, with an electric mixer, beat butter until creamy. With beaters running, gradually add sugar. Continue beating until mixture is light and fluffy. Add eggs, one at a time, beating well after each addition. Mix in vanilla. Add flour mixture and sour cream alternately to butter mixture, a little at a time. Beat well between each addition.

❖ In a medium bowl, mix together instant espresso powder and hot water. Add one third of cake batter to espresso mixture and combine thoroughly. Spoon half the plain batter into prepared pan, spreading evenly. Spoon espresso batter over plain batter, spread evenly. Spoon remaining plain batter over top and smooth gently with a spatula. Bake 55 to 60 minutes, or until a tester comes out clean. Place cake in pan on a rack and cool 30 minutes. Invert pan, remove cake and cool completely on rack.

❖ For Glaze: in a medium bowl, combine coffee and espresso powder. Stir until espresso powder is completely dissolved. Sift in powdered sugar and stir to blend thoroughly. Pour glaze over cake. Allow to sit 15 minutes before serving.

FRESH GINGER CAKE

serves eight

2	tablespoons butter, softened
2	tablespoons sugar
1	large egg
1/3	cup honey
2	tablespoons fresh ginger, grated
1	teaspoon lemon zest, grated
1	teaspoon vanilla extract
1 1/2	cups flour
1	teaspoon baking soda
3/4	teaspoon baking powder
1/2	teaspoon coriander
1/2	teaspoon cinnamon
1/8	teaspoon nutmeg
1/8	teaspoon salt
2	tablespoons crystallized ginger, finely chopped
1/2	cup buttermilk
2	teaspoons powdered sugar

Preheat oven to 350°.

❖ Grease and flour bottom and sides of an 8-inch round cake pan. Set aside.

❖ In a large bowl, beat butter and granulated sugar until light and fluffy. Beat in egg, honey, fresh ginger, lemon zest and vanilla. The mixture will curdle slightly.

❖ Sift together flour, baking soda, baking powder, coriander, cinnamon, nutmeg and salt. In a small bowl, toss crystallized ginger with 1/2 teaspoon of the dry ingredients to coat completely. Set aside. Alternately add remaining dry ingredients and buttermilk to butter mixture, beating well after each addition. Stir in crystallized ginger.

❖ Pour batter into prepared pan. Bake for 30 minutes, until a cake tester inserted in center comes out clean. Place on a rack and cool in pan for 10 minutes. Run a knife around the edge of the cake and turn it out of pan. Place right side up on rack and let cool completely. Sift powdered sugar over top just before serving.

Sift powdered sugar over a paper doily placed on top of cake for a special but effortless decoration.

HAZELNUT MOCHA MOUSSE ROLL
serves ten

Cake

4	ounces semi-sweet chocolate, chopped
1	tablespoon instant espresso powder
3	tablespoons boiling water
4	large eggs, separated
¾	cup sugar
2	tablespoons cocoa powder

Preheat oven to 350°.

❖ For Cake: butter bottom and sides of a 10x15-inch jelly roll pan. Line bottom of pan with parchment paper. Butter paper. Sprinkle paper-lined pan with flour, shaking to coat all sides evenly. Shake out excess flour. Melt chocolate in a double boiler over hot, not simmering, water. In a small bowl, combine espresso powder and water; stir until powder is dissolved. Stir coffee mixture into melted chocolate. Cool to room temperature.

❖ In a large bowl, beat egg yolks and sugar until thick and lemon-colored, about 5 minutes. Beat in chocolate mixture. In a separate bowl, beat egg whites until soft peaks form. Gently but thoroughly fold egg whites into chocolate mixture. Spread batter evenly in prepared pan. Smooth surface with spatula. Bake until top looks dry, about 12 to 15 minutes. Place pan on a rack. Cover cake with a slightly damp towel and cool completely.

❖ Run a small knife around sides of pan. Cover cake with a sheet of waxed paper and a baking sheet; invert cake onto baking sheet. Peel off parchment paper. Trim any hardened edges from sides of cake.

continued on page 231

Filling

1	6-ounce package hazelnuts
1 ¼	cups heavy cream
3	tablespoons hazelnut liqueur

Frosting

9	ounces semi-sweet chocolate
½	cup heavy cream

❖ For Filling: toast hazelnuts in oven about 10 minutes. Reserve 8 nuts for garnish. Finely chop remaining nuts. In a chilled bowl, with an electric mixer, beat cream and hazelnut liqueur until it holds soft peaks.

❖ For Frosting: place chocolate in the bowl of a food processor and chop very finely. Bring cream to a boil and add to chocolate. Process until chocolate melts and frosting is smooth.

❖ To Assemble: dust cake with cocoa powder and sprinkle with chopped hazelnuts. Spread whipped cream evenly over nuts, leaving a 1-inch border all around. Starting with a long side, roll up cake, lifting it with the waxed paper as you go, finishing with seam side down. Carefully transfer cake to a platter. Tear waxed paper into strips and tuck strips around bottom of cake on all sides to catch drips from frosting. Frost cake while frosting is still warm and runny. Garnish with whole hazelnuts. Remove waxed paper strips. Keep cake chilled.

❖ To Serve: cut cake with a serrated knife into 1 ½-inch slices. Place slices on their side to show off spiral pattern.

The cake portion of this recipe can be made a day in advance. Assemble and frost cake only 1 or 2 hours before serving.

BERRY PATCH SHORTCAKES
serves four

Shortcakes

1	cup flour
¼	cup cocoa powder
¼	cup sugar
1 ½	teaspoons baking powder
½	teaspoon baking soda
¼	teaspoon salt
¼	cup butter or margarine, chilled
½	cup heavy cream

Sauce

3	cups raspberries
2	tablespoons sugar
2	tablespoons raspberry liqueur

Garnish

⅔	cup heavy cream, chilled
2	tablespoons granulated sugar
2	tablespoons powdered sugar

Preheat oven to 425°.

❖   For Shortcakes: lightly butter a baking sheet. Sift together flour, cocoa powder, sugar, baking powder, baking soda and salt. Add butter and blend with a fork until mixture resembles coarse meal. Add cream and stir until mixture forms a dough. Form dough into 4 equal-sized shortcakes on prepared baking sheet, mound cakes slightly. Bake 12 to 15 minutes, or until a tester inserted in the center comes out clean. Transfer shortcakes to a rack to cool.

❖   For Sauce: in a large bowl, mash half the berries with a fork. Add 2 tablespoons sugar and the liqueur. Stir until sugar is dissolved. Stir in remaining berries.

❖   For Garnish: in a small, chilled bowl, beat cream until it holds soft peaks. Gradually sprinkle in granulated sugar and continue beating until cream holds stiff peaks.

❖   To Serve: using a serrated knife, carefully cut shortcakes in half, horizontally. With a spatula, place bottom halves on individual plates. Spoon some berry mixture over each bottom and top with whipped cream. Using a spatula, carefully place the tops over whipped cream. Place powdered sugar in a sieve and dust tops of shortcakes. Serve immediately.

PURPLE PLUM CHEESE TART
serves eight to ten

Tart Shell

1 1/2	cups flour
1	tablespoon sugar
1/8	teaspoon salt
1/2	cup butter or margarine, softened
1	egg yolk
1/4	teaspoon vanilla
2-3	tablespoons water

Filling

8	ounces cream cheese, softened
2	eggs
1/2	cup sugar
1/4	teaspoon cinnamon
1/4	teaspoon almond extract

Topping

1	cup water
1/2	cup sugar
20	purple plums, quartered

Preheat oven to 375°. Chilling time 1 hour and 30 minutes.

❖ For Tart Shell: in a medium bowl, combine flour, sugar and salt. Beat together butter and egg yolk with a fork. Add to flour mixture. Add vanilla and 2 tablespoons water. Using an electric mixer, blend until combined. Add remaining tablespoon water if dough is too dry. Form dough into a ball, dust with flour and refrigerate 30 minutes. On a lightly floured surface, roll dough into a circle. Line bottom and sides of a 9-inch springform pan with dough. Trim excess dough with a knife. Prick bottom of pastry shell with a fork. Bake until lightly browned, about 15 minutes. Cool in pan on a rack.

❖ For Filling: in a large bowl, combine cream cheese, eggs, 1/2 cup sugar, cinnamon and almond extract. Beat with an electric mixer until smooth. Pour filling into cooled pastry shell. Bake until filling is set, about 25 minutes. Place pan on a rack to cool.

❖ For Topping: in a medium pan, bring water and sugar to a boil. Add quartered plums. Simmer until plums are just tender, about 2 minutes. Remove plums with a slotted spoon; drain and cool. Continue boiling syrup until thickened and reduced to 1/3 cup. Cool syrup.

❖ To Assemble: arrange plums decoratively on baked cheese filling. Spoon syrup over plums. Refrigerate tart at least 1 hour. Remove tart from springform pan. Serve chilled.

LEMON-GINGER CHEESECAKE
serves twelve

Crust

30	gingersnap cookies
2	tablespoons sugar
1	tablespoon lemon zest, grated
¼	cup butter, melted

Lemon Curd

¼	teaspoon unflavored gelatin
1	teaspoon water
½	cup sugar
1	tablespoon lemon zest, grated
¼	cup lemon juice, freshly squeezed
3	egg yolks
6	tablespoons butter

Preheat oven to 350°. Chilling time overnight.

❖ For Crust: lightly oil a 9-inch springform pan. In a blender or food processor, finely grind gingersnaps with sugar and lemon zest. Add butter and blend well. Pat crumb mixture into bottom of prepared pan. Place on middle rack of preheated oven and bake 12 minutes. Cool on a wire rack.

❖ For Lemon Curd: sprinkle gelatin over cold water in a small bowl. Let stand 10 minutes to soften. In a blender or food processor, blend sugar with lemon zest until zest is as fine as sugar. Transfer to a small, heavy saucepan. Add lemon juice, egg yolks and butter. Stir over medium heat until very thick, about 5 minutes; do not boil. Remove from heat, add gelatin and stir to dissolve. Cool completely, stirring frequently, about 1 hour.

continued on page 235

Lemon Curd may be made up to 1 week in advance and stored in the refrigerator. It is also heavenly spread on toast in the morning!

Filling

1	tablespoon plus 1 teaspoon unflavored gelatin
¼	cup cold water
¾	cup sugar
1	1-inch piece fresh ginger, peeled
	zest from 2 lemons, grated
¼	teaspoon salt
3	egg yolks
¾	cup milk
12	ounces cream cheese, at room temperature
⅓	cup lemon juice, freshly squeezed
1½	cups heavy cream, chilled

❖ For Filling: in a small bowl, sprinkle gelatin over cold water. Let stand 10 minutes to soften. Place sugar, ginger, lemon zest and salt in blender or food processor and process until zest is as fine as sugar. Add egg yolks and blend until light and fluffy. Scald milk in medium saucepan. With processor running, add milk through feed tube and blend well. Return mixture to saucepan. Stir over medium-low heat until mixture thickens, about 12 minutes. Do not boil. Add gelatin mixture to custard and stir until dissolved. Strain into bowl, pressing on solids with back of spoon. Refrigerate until cool and thickened, but not set, about 20 minutes.

❖ Blend cream cheese and lemon juice in blender or processor until smooth. Add custard and blend until uniformly mixed.

❖ In a large bowl, whip cream to soft peaks. Gently fold in filling mixture. Pour half of filling over crust. Drop half of lemon curd by tablespoonfuls over filling. Swirl mixtures together, using tip of knife. Add remaining filling, drop remaining curd and swirl as before. Refrigerate overnight.

❖ To Serve: run a knife around side of cake pan and release pan sides. Cut into wedges and serve immediately.

WHITE CHOCOLATE RASPBERRY CHEESECAKE
serves eight

Crust

1	cup vanilla wafer crumbs
$\frac{1}{2}$	cup almonds, ground
2	tablespoons sugar
$\frac{1}{8}$	teaspoon almond extract
3	tablespoons butter or margarine, melted

Filling

4	ounces white chocolate, chopped
16	ounces cream cheese
3	large eggs
$\frac{3}{4}$	cup sugar
2	teaspoons flour
1	teaspoon vanilla

Glaze

$\frac{1}{4}$	cup heavy cream
4	ounces white chocolate, chopped

Preheat oven to 350°. Chilling time 8 hours.

❖ For Crust: combine all ingredients in a small bowl. Mix with a fork until mixture resembles coarse crumbs. Press into bottom of an 8 or 9-inch springform pan. Bake 10 minutes. Cool completely. Reduce oven temperature to 325°.

❖ For Filling: melt white chocolate in double boiler. Cool to lukewarm. In a medium bowl, beat cream cheese with electric mixer until smooth. Add eggs, one at a time, mixing well after each addition. Mix in sugar, flour and vanilla. Gently but thoroughly blend in melted white chocolate. Pour filling over crust. Bake until cheesecake is firm around edges, but still moves slightly in center when gently shaken, about 40 minutes. Cool completely. Cover and refrigerate 8 hours or overnight.

❖ For Glaze: in a small saucepan, bring cream to simmer over low heat. Add chocolate and stir until smooth. Spread glaze evenly over top of cheesecake. Refrigerate until set. Cake may be made ahead to this point up to 2 days in advance.

continued on page 237

12 ounces frozen raspberries

½ cup white wine

⅓ cup sugar

fresh raspberries for garnish (optional)

❖ For Sauce: thaw raspberries in a sieve placed over a bowl, reserving juice. In a small saucepan, boil wine and sugar until reduced to ¼ cup, about 10 minutes. Puree thawed berries in a food processor. Press puree through a sieve to remove seeds. Sweeten puree with 2 tablespoons each wine syrup and reserved raspberry juice, adding more to taste.

❖ To Serve. spoon a pool of raspberry sauce onto individual plates. Slice cheesecake and place on top of sauce. Drizzle more sauce over top, if desired. Garnish plates with fresh berries.

PRALINE BRIE
serves six

1 8-inch wheel of brie cheese

2 tablespoons butter or margarine

4 tablespoons brown sugar

1 cup pecans, chopped

Preheat oven to 275°.

❖ Place brie on a baking sheet. Bake until soft, 15 to 20 minutes. Melt butter in a small saucepan. Add brown sugar and stir until dissolved. Stir in pecans. Place brie on a serving tray and pour pecan mixture over, letting it dribble over sides. Serve surrounded by crackers and fresh fruit such as sliced apples and pears, strawberries and grapes.

Desserts

APPLE PIE AMERICANA
serves eight

Crust
- 1½ cups flour
- ½ cup vegetable oil
- 2 tablespoons milk, very cold
- 1½ teaspoons sugar
- 1 teaspoon salt

Filling
- 6 cups apples, peeled, cored and thinly sliced
- ¾ cup sugar
- 3 tablespoons flour
- ¾ teaspoon ground cinnamon
- ½ teaspoon ground nutmeg

Topping
- ½ cup flour
- ½ cup sugar
- ½ cup butter

Preheat oven to 350°.

❖ For Crust: in a large bowl, mix together flour, oil, milk, sugar and salt until evenly blended. Pat mixture into a 9-inch pie pan, spreading dough evenly over bottom and up sides. Crimp edges of dough around perimeter of pan.

❖ For Filling: toss apple slices with sugar, flour, cinnamon and nutmeg. Spread evenly in unbaked pie shell.

❖ For Topping: mix together flour, sugar and butter until evenly distributed and crumbly in texture. Sprinkle over apple filling.

❖ Place pie on a baking sheet on middle rack of preheated oven. Bake 60 minutes, or until apples are tender. Serve warm with vanilla ice cream, if desired.

Experiment with different varieties of Washington's famous apples. Golden Delicious, Granny Smith and McIntosh are all good cooking apples.

ALMOND À LA TARTE
serves eight

Pastry

1	cup flour
1	tablespoon sugar
½	cup butter or margarine, softened
1	teaspoon vanilla
¼	teaspoon almond extract

Filling

1	cup sliced almonds
¾	cup sugar
¾	cup heavy cream
2	teaspoons orange liqueur
¼	teaspoon salt
2	drops almond extract

Chilling time 1 hour. Preheat oven to 400°.

❖ For Crust: butter a 9 or 10-inch springform pan. In a medium bowl, mix flour and sugar. Add butter, vanilla and almond extract. Blend with an electric mixer until mixture begins to form a ball. Press dough into bottom and halfway up sides of prepared pan. Refrigerate 1 hour. Bake crust until lightly browned, 10 to 15 minutes. Place pan on a wire rack to cool.

❖ For Filling: thoroughly combine all ingredients in a medium bowl. Pour into baked pastry shell. Bake until filling is set, 45 to 55 minutes. Filling should be caramelized when fully baked. Cool completely. Cut into wedges to serve.

CRANBERRY CRUMB TART
serves ten

Tart Shell

½   cup butter, chilled

1 ⅓ cups flour

1   tablespoon sugar

¼   teaspoon salt

4   tablespoons ice water

Chilling time at least 1 hour and 30 minutes. Preheat oven to 425°.

❖   For Tart Shell: cut butter into ½-inch cubes and place in a food processor with flour, sugar and salt. Pulse on-off quickly until mixture resembles coarse meal. With motor running, add 4 tablespoons ice water; mix just until dough forms a ball. Wrap in plastic and flatten into a disc. Refrigerate at least 30 minutes.

❖   On a floured surface, roll dough into a 14-inch round. Dust dough lightly with flour and fold into quarters. Center over a 10-inch tart pan with removable bottom. Open up pastry and press against sides of pan, folding down excess to reinforce sides. Cover with plastic wrap and refrigerate at least 1 hour, or overnight.

❖   Line pastry with foil and fill with pie weights or dried beans. Bake 20 minutes. Remove foil and weights; prick bottom and sides all over with a fork. Bake 5 to 8 minutes more, until crust is golden brown. Reduce oven temperature to 325°.

continued on page 241

Filling

1	cup fresh cranberries
¾	cup sugar, divided
½	cup dried currants
2	tablespoons dark rum
2	Golden Delicious apples, peeled, quartered and thinly sliced
1½	teaspoons lemon zest, grated
1	tablespoon lemon juice
½	teaspoon cinnamon

Crumb Topping

1	cup flour
¾	cup sugar
½	teaspoon salt
8	tablespoons butter, chilled

❖ For Filling: coarsely chop cranberries with ¼ cup sugar and transfer mixture to a fine sieve set over a bowl; drain for 1 hour. In another small bowl, combine currants and rum; let stand 1 hour.

❖ In large bowl, combine apples, remaining ½ cup sugar, lemon zest, lemon juice and cinnamon. Add the cranberry mixture (with excess liquid pressed out) and the currant mixture.

❖ For Crumb Topping: combine flour, sugar and salt in food processor. Cut butter into ½-inch cubes and add to mixture. Pulse on-off quickly until mixture resembles coarse meal and clumps together when pressed with fingers.

❖ Spread filling over baked shell, mounding slightly in center. Using fingertips, lightly squeeze topping into clumps and drop over berries. Do not press topping onto fruit.

❖ Bake tart until topping is golden brown, about 40 minutes. Serve at room temperature. The tart will keep up to 3 days in refrigerator.

RASPBERRY TART
serves eight

Crust

1	cup walnuts, ground
½	cup butter, softened
3	tablespoons sugar
1½	cups flour
1	egg yolk, beaten
½	teaspoon vanilla extract

Filling

6	ounces semi-sweet chocolate chips
2	cups fresh raspberries
1	package unflavored gelatin
2	tablespoons raspberry liqueur
¾	cup red currant jelly
1	cup heavy cream
2	tablespoons powdered sugar

Chilling time 1 hour. Preheat oven to 350°.

❖ For Crust: place walnuts, butter, sugar, flour, egg yolk and vanilla extract in a food processor with metal blade. Pulse on-off several times until just blended. Press dough evenly into bottom and sides of a 9-inch tart pan with removable bottom. Chill 1 hour. Bake crust in preheated oven 15 minutes. Cool in pan on wire rack.

❖ For Filling: melt chocolate chips in top of a double boiler over simmering water. Spread melted chips evenly over bottom of cooled crust, being careful not to drip chocolate on the edges. Arrange raspberries over crust in concentric circles, starting from the outside and working in.

❖ In a small saucepan, combine gelatin and liqueur. Let stand 15 minutes. Add currant jelly. Stir over low heat until smooth and gelatin is dissolved. Remove from heat, cool slightly, and brush gently over berries using a soft pastry brush. (You may not need all the glaze.) Let stand a few minutes to set. Refrigerate until 30 minutes before serving.

❖ Whip cream until soft peaks form, gradually adding powdered sugar.

❖ Cut tart into wedges and serve with a dollop of whipped cream.

STRAWBERRY ALMOND TORTE

serves eight

Ingredients

1½ cups slivered almonds, toasted

½ cup sugar

1 cup flour

¼ teaspoon salt

½ cup butter (not margarine), chilled

12 ounces white chocolate, grated

2 cups heavy cream, divided

3 cups fresh strawberries, washed, hulled and cut into thick slices

Garnish

8 whole strawberries

Preheat oven to 375°. Chilling time 3 hours or overnight.

❖ For Torte: place almonds and sugar in food processor and process until very finely ground. Add flour and salt, process until blended. Cut butter into cubes, add to nut mixture and process until dough holds together. Wrap dough in plastic and refrigerate at least 1 hour or overnight.

❖ Line 2 large baking sheets with parchment paper. Using an 8-inch cake pan as a guide, trace 3 circles on parchment. Divide pastry into 3 equal parts and pat evenly into circles. Bake until golden brown, 8 to 10 minutes. Cool 2 minutes, then cut each circle into 8 wedges. Cool completely.

❖ For Mousse: place chocolate in a large bowl. In a small saucepan, scald ½ cup cream. Pour cream over chocolate and stir until melted. Cool to room temperature. In a separate bowl, whip remaining cream to form soft peaks. Carefully fold whipped cream into chocolate mixture. Cover and refrigerate until set, 3 hours or overnight.

❖ To Assemble: place 1 circle of wedges on a serving platter. Using a pastry bag fitted with a large star tip, pipe mousse onto each wedge to cover. Top mousse with half the sliced berries. Top with a second circle of wedges; make sure wedges line up with first circle. Repeat piping of mousse and top with remaining sliced berries. Place remaining wedges around top. Garnish with remaining mousse and whole berries. Refrigerate at least 1 hour.

APPLE BREAD PUDDING WITH CIDER SAUCE
serves eight

Bread Pudding

½ cup raisins

¼ cup rum

6 tablespoons butter, divided

3 cups apples, peeled, cored and sliced ¼-inch thick

¾ cup sugar, divided

3½ cups firm-textured white bread, cubed

3 large eggs

2 cups milk

1 teaspoon vanilla extract

¼ teaspoon nutmeg

Preheat oven to 375°.

❖ Butter a 6 to 8 cup baking dish. Place raisins in a medium-sized bowl. Heat rum and pour over raisins. Set aside.

❖ Melt 2 tablespoons butter in a large skillet over medium heat. Add apples and sauté, turning frequently, for about 5 minutes, until apples begin to turn golden. Add 3 tablespoons sugar and sauté for 3 minutes longer, until sugar begins to caramelize. Transfer apples to bowl with raisins.

❖ Add remaining 4 tablespoons butter to skillet, reduce heat to low and add bread cubes. Toss for a few minutes until evenly coated with butter. Remove from heat. Scatter half the apple-raisin mixture over bottom of baking dish. Cover with half the bread cubes. Repeat layers.

❖ Lightly beat eggs and ½ cup sugar. Scald milk. Slowly pour scalded milk in a thin stream into egg mixture, stirring constantly with a whisk. Add vanilla and nutmeg. Pour mixture over apples and bread. Set baking dish in a larger pan and add boiling water to come halfway up sides of baking dish. Place in middle of oven and bake 45 minutes, until top is crusty and golden. Serve warm with Cider Sauce.

continued on page 245

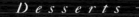

Cider Sauce

2½   cups apple cider
½   cup sugar
2   teaspoons cornstarch
⅓   cup light rum

❖   For Cider Sauce: set aside 2 tablespoons cider. Boil remaining cider until reduced to 1 cup. Add sugar and cook over medium heat until sugar is dissolved. Dissolve cornstarch in reserved cider. Stir cornstarch mixture into hot cider mixture. Bring to a boil, reduce heat, and simmer until sauce turns clear and thickens, stirring often. Add rum. Serve warm sauce with bread pudding.

APPLE BLACKBERRY CRISP
serves six

Filling

6   apples, Golden Delicious or Granny Smith
2   cups blackberries, fresh or frozen
½   cup sugar
2   tablespoons flour

Topping

½   cup rolled oats
½   cup flour
½   cup chopped nuts, (optional)
⅓   cup butter, melted
⅓   cup brown sugar
1   teaspoon cinnamon

Preheat oven to 350°.

❖   For Filling: butter a 9x13-inch baking dish. Peel and core apples. Cut into thin slices. Place apples in prepared baking dish. Top with blackberries. (If using frozen berries, do not thaw first.) Sprinkle with sugar and flour.

❖   For Topping: combine all ingredients in a small bowl until crumbly.

❖   Sprinkle topping evenly over filling. Bake until fruit is soft and bubbly and topping is browned, about 35 to 40 minutes. Serve warm, topped with vanilla ice cream or whipped cream.

RHUBARBERRY CRISP
serves four to six

Filling

3	cups fresh rhubarb
1½	cups raspberries or strawberries
¾	cup sugar
3	tablespoons flour

Topping

1	cup flour
½	cup brown sugar
1	teaspoon baking powder
¼	teaspoon salt
6	tablespoons butter, softened
⅓	cup chopped nuts, (optional)

Preheat oven to 350°.

❖ For Filling: butter a 9-inch square baking dish. Cut rhubarb into 1-inch pieces. Place in prepared pan. Top with berries. (If using frozen berries, do not thaw first.) Sprinkle fruit with sugar and flour.

❖ For Topping: in a small bowl, combine flour, sugar, baking powder and salt. Add butter and mix with fingertips until mixture resembles coarse crumbs. Add nuts.

❖ Sprinkle topping evenly over filling. Bake until fruit is soft and bubbly and topping is browned, about 35 to 40 minutes. Serve warm with vanilla ice cream or whipped cream.

Filling

35	Italian plums
½	cup sugar
2	tablespoons flour
2	large eggs, lightly beaten

Topping

see Rhubarberry Crisp

PLUM CRISP
serves four to six

Preheat oven to 350°.

❖ For Filling: butter a 9-inch square baking dish. Pit plums and cut into quarters. Place plums in prepared dish. In a small bowl, combine sugar, flour and eggs, mixing well. Pour over fruit.

❖ For Topping: follow instructions for Rhubarberry Crisp, increasing baking time to 45 to 50 minutes.

WHIDBEY ISLAND SOUFFLÉS
serves four

Ingredients

1   cup blackberries, raspberries or loganberries, rinsed

9   tablespoons sugar, divided

4   large eggs, separated

Preheat oven to 425°.

❖   In a heavy saucepan, cook berries with 2 tablespoons sugar over low heat until mixture is slightly syrupy, about 5 minutes. Puree the mixture and strain it through a fine sieve to remove seeds.

❖   Butter four ½-cup ramekins and dust with 1 tablespoon sugar. With an electric mixer, beat egg yolks until they are thick and pale. Gently fold in ½ cup puree. Reserve any remaining puree for another use.

❖   With clean beaters, in a large bowl, beat egg whites until foamy. Add remaining 6 tablespoons sugar, a little at a time, beating until whites just hold stiff peaks. Stir ½ cup whites into yolk mixture, then fold in remaining whites gently but thoroughly.

❖   Divide mixture among the ramekins and set them in a baking pan. Add enough boiling water to the pan to come 1 inch up sides of ramekins.

❖   Place pan in preheated oven and bake 13 to 15 minutes, until puffed and golden brown. Place each ramekin on a dessert plate and serve immediately.

FROZEN ESPRESSO CREAM
serves six

2   cups heavy cream

2   cups half and half

1   cup sugar

¼   cup Bristol Cream sherry

3   tablespoons instant espresso powder

⅛   teaspoon salt

Freezing time 8 hours.

❖   In a large bowl, combine cream, half and half and sugar. Stir until sugar is dissolved. Stir in sherry, espresso powder and salt until thoroughly combined.

❖   Pour mixture into an ice cream maker and freeze according to manufacturer's instructions. Serve immediately, or place in a covered plastic container and let stand in freezer 8 hours to allow flavors to blend. Thirty minutes before serving, remove from freezer and place in refrigerator to soften.

CHOCOLATE ORANGE SORBET
serves six

Ingredients

¾   cup sugar

⅔   cup cocoa powder

1½   cups water

1   ounce bittersweet or semi-sweet chocolate

¼   cup orange juice, freshly squeezed

1   tablespoon orange zest, grated

Freezing time overnight.

❖   Combine sugar and cocoa powder in a medium saucepan over low heat. Slowly stir in water. Chop chocolate and add to pan. Cook until chocolate melts and sugar dissolves. Increase heat to medium-high and boil 1 minute, stirring constantly. Pour mixture into a medium bowl, stir in orange juice and zest. Refrigerate until well chilled.

❖   Transfer mixture to an ice cream maker and process according to manufacturer's instructions. Cover and freeze overnight to allow flavors to mellow.

FRUIT SORBET WITH BLACKBERRY COULIS

serves eight

Pear Sorbet

4	ripe pears
½ - ¾	cup sugar
¼	cup lemon juice, freshly squeezed
3	tablespoons pear brandy

Strawberry Sorbet

5	cups strawberries, hulled
½ - ¾	cup powdered sugar
2	tablespoons lemon juice, freshly squeezed
1	tablespoon raspberry brandy

Blackberry Coulis

¼	cup sugar
¼	cup water
1½	cups blackberries

Garnish

mint sprigs

Freezing time 8 hours.

❖ For Pear Sorbet: peel, core and cut pears into medium chunks. In a food processor, puree pears, ½ cup sugar, lemon juice and pear brandy until smooth. Taste and add more sugar, as needed, depending on sweetness of pears. Pour puree into an ice cream maker and freeze according to manufacturer's instructions. Place frozen sorbet in a covered plastic container in freezer. Transfer to refrigerator 1 hour before serving.

❖ For Strawberry Sorbet: in a food processor, puree strawberries in 2 batches until smooth. Press puree through a fine strainer into a large bowl. Discard seeds. Sift powdered sugar over strawberry puree and blend thoroughly. Stir in lemon juice and raspberry brandy. Pour mixture into an ice cream maker and freeze according to manufacturer's instructions. Place frozen sorbet in a covered plastic container in freezer. Transfer to refrigerator 1 hour before serving.

❖ For Blackberry Coulis: in a small saucepan, combine sugar and water. Boil over high heat for 3 minutes. Chill well.

❖ In food processor or blender, puree blackberries. Strain through a fine sieve and discard seeds. Gradually stir chilled sugar syrup into blackberry puree, until desired sweetness is reached. Cover coulis and refrigerate.

❖ To Assemble: swirl 2 tablespoons of coulis on 8 cold plates. Top with small scoop of each sorbet. Garnish with mint sprigs.

—Acknowledgements—

The Junior League of Seattle thanks its members, families and friends who have contributed to this book. It is our sincere hope that no one has been inadvertently overlooked.

Bartley Aanenson
Carmen Abadilla
Ginger Ackerley
Judy Addington
Donna Addison
Lynn Addison
Peggy Agress
Carol Allen
Jane Allen
Laura Allen
Lynn Allison
Tom Allison
Louise Altick
Betsy Amento
Christie Anderson
Kathryn Anderson
Victoria Anderson
Lynn Anglin
Margery Armstrong
Julie Arnevick
Leslie Astrup
Diane Atkinson
Cheryl Avery
❖
Anne Barker
Joan Bauer
Anne Baumgartner
John Baxter
Kay Baxter
Julie Bayless
Peggy Beam
Helen Becker
Julie Bell
Lauren Bennett
Maureen Benoliel
Maggie Bentley

Patricia Bentson
Jennifer Berg
Janet Berman
Jo Berry
Louise Berry
Lori Berst
Tracy Beyer
Catherine Blanchard
Mary Blazek
Jina Bonime
Karen Booth
Margaret Bordeaux
Susan Bordner
Leslie Bowlin
Margaret Breen
Beth Brewer
J.P. Brigham
Fran Buckley
Georgie Bunch
Gladys Burkhardt
Lou Bush
❖
Shary Cahill
Sue Caldwell
Melanie Callander
Cyndy Carfi
Sally Carman
Glynis Carrosino
Susan Carson
Anna Carter
Sally Casey
Susan Cashman
Sarah Cater
Luanne Caylor
Carrie Caylor
Debora Centioli

Sallie Chaney
Judy Chapman
Susan Chin
Deborah Chvila-Dols
Cary Clark
Marge Clark
Debbie Cleveland
Elaine Clifford
Pam Cobb
Lesli Ann Cone
Mary Connell
Jon Connell
Sue Conrad
Molly Coumbs
Debbie Covey
Sarah Cox
Lorrie Cross
Barbara Crutcher
Cynthia Cunningham
Melanie Currier
Becky Curtis
❖
Laurie D'Alessandro
Chris Daher
Ann Danford
Lisa Dangelmaier
Debbie Daniels
Agnes Davis
Lynn Dawson
Lola Deane
Christy DeNova
Catherine Dietrich
Ray Dittamore
Jacque Doane
Kathe Dobbs
Julie Doces

Julie Donnan
Marty Donworth
Donna Dornes
Sue Draper
Carol Driver
Pam Drugge
Patricia Dunbar
❖
Carolyn Eley
Donna Ellis
Kathy Erickson
Pam Eshelman
Judy Evans
Cathy Evans
Louise Everett
❖
Melissa Fairley
Marlene Fallquist
Colleen Farris-Weaver
Cheryl Fick
Kathy Fishman
Betty Fitzpatrick
Susan Fletcher
Nancy Flohr
Mary Ann Flynn
Lucy Bauer Footlik
Marc Footlik
Molly Fox
Patricia Frankland
Kari Freeman
Michele Fricke
Beverly Fuhs
❖
Kathy Galt
Joanna Gardiner
Deb Giannola

Karen Gibbons
Jane Gibson
Valerie Giesbrecht
Michelle Gilliland
Janet Givler
Susan Gjefle
Linda Goodrick
Marsha Gopal
Robyn Grad
Paula Graef
Evelyn Graham
Kathryn Grant
Elizabeth Greathouse
Mary Green
Andrea Gregg
Jean Griffin
Betsy Grimes
Robin Guterson
❖
Barbara Hack
Cindy Hales
Cynthia Hall
Georgia Hall
Dorothy Halliday
Laura Halliday
Scott Halliday
Linda Halverson
Shan Hammer
Donna Hampton
Jennifer Hand
Claudia Hansen
Shari Hardy
Karen Harkness
Linda Harrison
Libby Harvey
Barbara Haspedis

Jean Hassenger
Chera Hassinger
Bob Haynie
Kris Hegger
Chris Hennig-Agatep
Cindy Henning
Mary Herche
Ann Herron
Joan Hibbs
Luke Hill
Margot Hill
Kris Hodge
Marge Hoefer
Margery Hokonson
Debra Holland
Teresa Holland
Gina Holt
Patricia Honnen
Alan Hughes
Bill Hughlett
Kayce Hughlett
Gratia Huxley
❖
Thomas Ingalls
Susan Ishmael
❖
Catharine Jacobsen
Katy Janicki
Beverly Jefferson
Debbie Jennings
Marge Johnson
Robert Johnson
Christina Johnson
Holly Johnson
Mary Lou Johnson
Janet Jones

JoAnne Jones
Judy Jones
Karen Jones
De Jurkovich
Valerie Jusela
❖
Janet Keeney
Jeannene Kelly
Libby King
Marnie Kirchner
Carol Kiriluk
Pam Kirzinger
Carolyn Kitchell
Lynn Kloppenburg
Lisa Knapp
Kelley Koch
Sharon Kohls
Laura Koszarek
❖
Patti L'Heureux
Linda Lake
Nancy Jo Langrehr
Ann Lantz
Susan Larson
Betsy LaTorre
Pam Lee
Elizabeth Leider
Judy Leithe
Louise Lemert
Kathryn Lewis
Roma Lindbloom
Carol Linde
Cathi Lindstrom
Patricia Little
B.J. Livingston
Chris Lizee

— Acknowledgements —

Elizabeth Lochte
Laurie Lorenzen
Deborah Loucks
Jenette Low

❖

Linda MacGeorge
Lisa MacGeorge
Paula MacGeorge
Maria Mackey
Pam Macki
Susan MacLellan
June MacLellan
Helen Mandley
Ann Marols
Ann Marsh
Jeva Marshall
Cindy Masin
Martha Matcovich
Cris Matthew
Wanda Matthews
Judyann Maus
Janet McClure
Caron McCune
Ann McCutchan
Diane McDonald
Marsha McGillivray
Martha McKay
Sharon Meeks
Nancy Menzies-Vaessen
Bonnie Mickelson
Jean Miller
Jamie Milne
Susan Minahan
Bliss Moore
Kim Moore
Merry Moos
Parmalee Moos
Terry Moos
Terry Moreman

Pat Moriarty
Dana Morris
Heidi Morris
Leslie Morris
Marla Moss
Marsha Moss
Peggy-Paige Most
Molly Mowe
Jeanie Mowrer
Esther Murdock
Jarvis Murphy
Joy Murray
Kacy Murray

❖

John Nashu
Nancy Nashu
Cindy Neal
Jenny Nelson
June Nessler
Debbie Neudorfer
Kay Nichols
Lynn Nichols
Sherry Northrop
Sue Norton

❖

Kerry Oldenburg
Drea Olmstead
Kimberly Olmstead
Marie Olmstead
Gail Orendorff
Sara Orr
Anne Ossewaarde
Kirk Ossewaarde
Linda Ozawa

❖

Laurie Padden
Wendy Pamer
Jo-Ann Parrish
Sandra Parry

Lisa Pascualy
Sandy Patchin
Virginia Patty
Colleen Payne
Mary Margaret Pearson
Susan Pearson
Carolyn Puckenpaugh
Lana Peta
Betsey Peters
Robyn Peterson
Hollyce Phillips
Nancy Piantanida
Mavis Piper
Susan Plunkett
Katherine Pomeroy
Kathryn Pratt
Lindsay Price
Adam Puente

❖

Terri Quick

❖

Kit Rasmussen
Mary Reichman
Meg Reid
Helen Reiley
Susan Reiter
Sara Reynolds
Gail Richards
Barbara Riede
Barbara Ries
Gail Roberts
Kathleen Ann Roberts
Pat Roberts
Cathy Rodden
Margie Rose
Norma Rosenthal
Laura Roszarek
Patti Roth
Amy Rudolf

Elizabeth Rudolf
Kathy Rumburger

❖

Ernie Sampera
Karen Schmidt
Cindi Schoettler
Lisa Schoettler
Jean Schuster
Molly Sears
Rone Seeks
Marsha Seeley
Marie Shanley
Diane Shapiro
Kimberly Shaplen
Marianna Sheehan
Jean Sheeran
Betsy Sherrow
Vici Shoemaker
Lynne Shrum
Kathy Shultz
Kia Slan
Betsy Silva
Ann Simmons
Susan Simmons
Sue Simonds
Julie Sirotak
Kathleen Skinner
Carol Smith
Christy Smith
Colleen Smith
Diane Smith
Helen Smith
Mary Smith
Molly Smith
Robert Smith
Diane Snellings
Sara Soracco
Margaret Spickard
Ann Spiess

Ann Stables
Maggie Stalcup
Laurie Stanton
Grace Steers
Linda Stemer
Candace Stern
Margo Stevenson
Pam Stewart
Pam Stokesbury
Cee-Cee Stromer
Daisy Struble
Barbara Sulman
Jane Summerfelt
Kerry Sussex
Kathy Sutcliffe
Darci Swanson
Sandy Sweeney

❖

Nona Tagliavento
Celia Talkington
Maren Tall
Susan Tapper
Nancy Tarbert
Ann Tarpchinoff
Lynn Taylor
Jamie Terman
Grace Thompson
Sally Thomson
Vikki Thornton
Tricia Tiano
Christy Timberlake
Patricia Timm
Sue Tong
Gayle Tonkin
Diane Torrance
Sarah Tousley
Enid Trevithick
Wendy Truitt
Debbie Tucigisser

Nancy Turnure
Rick Turnure
Terri Turnure
Tom Turnure

❖

Judy Uyemura

❖

Donna Van Dusor
Carol Van Dyk
Karen Vander Hoek
Ann Vanderwall
Kathryn Volk

❖

Mrs. James Wade
Judith Walcutt
Phil Walter
Marilyn Ward
Jan Wasser
Linda Watkins
Peggy Watt
Dorothy Wayne
Susan Weatherman
Randi Weber
Carol Weigand
Ginger Whelan
Karen Whitney
Karen Wickstrand
Betsy Wilcox
Paul Wilcox
Celia Williams
LaVonne Williams
Nancy Williams
Debbi Wilson
Nancy Wilson
Donna Winblade
Mitzi Winchell
Mary Jane Windes
Lowell Winkler
Ruth Winkler

Debbie Winn
Kay Wippu
Nancy Woolridge
Betty Wyman

❖

Cindy Zech
Darcey Zimmerman
Allison Zito
JoAnn Zsitvay

❖

Special Thanks to:

Arthur Andersen
Canterbury Cuisine
The Columbia Winery
DeLaurenti Market
Dirks & Daniel
The Galley Slave
The Main Attraction
Nordstrom
The Paper Tree
Restaurants Unlimited
Stockpot Soups
Sunshine Kitchens
Sunwest Enterprises
Techna Print
Kirsten Meyer of
Unisource
Mr. & Mrs. John Baxter
Mr. & Mrs. Gerard V.
Centioli
Mr. & Mrs. Robert
Simonds
Mr. & Mrs. Tom Turnure

Northwest artist Heidi-Marie Blackwell attended the University of Washington, where she received a Bachelor of Fine Arts in Graphic Design with a second major in Painting, studying with Norman Lundin. She studied in France and traveled extensively in Europe. Graduating from the UW in 1976, Heidi-Marie moved to Los Angeles, where she focused primarily on the design of annual reports and collateral corporate marketing materials. After seven years she returned to Seattle and spent the following ten years building her graphic design business, Blackwell Design, painting infrequently. In time, gallery and corporate exhibitions and commissions began to provide a shift. Blackwell Design expanded to become Blackwell Studios. Heidi-Marie now primarily works in painting and takes on design when time and interest allow.

The focus of her painting in the last decade has been primarily "places" to be that define a specific atmosphere and represent people in their absence. Design has crossed over into Heidi-Marie's painting. In her opinion, good design requires a process of simplification and organization of key elements. In her painting, balance and eye-flow are controlled by their "just so" placement. The overall image defines an atmosphere, through color and surface texture, which relays time of day, season, mood, etc. A person's chosen environment can tell the viewer more about that person, present or absent, than a traditional portrait.

We the Junior League of Seattle have expanded our product line to include:

- **Notecards** (an assortment of 8 images with recipes from the cookbook plus envelopes).

- **Gift Enclosure Cards** (an assortment of 11 images from the cookbook plus envelopes).

For pricing and shipping information please call our hotline: (206) 860-7501 or fax your request to (206) 324-0811.

Profits from the sale of this cookbook are used to support community projects of the Junior League of Seattle, Inc.

The Junior League of Seattle is an organization of women committed to promoting voluntarism, developing the potential of women, and improving the community through the effective action and leadership of trained volunteers. It's purpose is exclusively educational and charitable.

JLS devotes more than 100,000 volunteer hours each year to community projects in the areas of education, the arts, human services and family, children's and women's issues.